Feng Shui:

Art and Harmony of Place

Feng Shui:
Art and Harmony of Place

Johndennis Govert

Daikakuji Publications
Phoenix, Arizona

Daikakuji Publications
Post Office Box 44035
Phoenix, Arizona 85064-4035

Printed in the United States of America

ISBN: 0-9637254-8-3

Library of Congress Catalog Card Number: 93-090551

Cover art work: Howard Bernstein
Cover Design: Joan Eidinger
Back cover photography: Renata Golden
CAD illustrations and floor plans: James J. Sullivan
Chinese calligraphy and *Tao Te Ching* translations: Johndennis Govert

Printed on acid-free paper

Dedication

To my parents, John William and Marita Terese Govert:
May I return a portion of your great kindnesses to help others.

Acknowledgements

Many and deep thanks
to Howard Bernstein for the artwork for the front cover;
to Joan Eidinger for the design and layout of the cover;
to Renata Golden for critical review, editing, layout and back cover photography;
to Richard Mann for unlimited computer patience;
to George Drum for printing;
to James J. Sullivan for CAD illustrations and floor plans;
to Ann Marchiony for marketing strategy;
to Matsuoka Soyu Roshi for Zen insights and back cover inkan;
to Professor Chong Lu-sheng for scholarly teachings;
to Goswami Kriyananda for astrological training and many blessings;
to Master Quan Guan-liang for *qi gong* & no-mind teachings;
to my wife, Anita Govert, for endless patience and encouragement;
and to all the wisdom teachers who have ever taught me.
May I return a portion of all your great kindnesses to help others.

Table of Contents

Feng Shui: Finding the Roots of Heaven At Home

"This president was the biggest egomaniac. No one could work with him. The company went belly up in six months!" That was the realty agent's preamble as he, my client, and I walked into the vacant lobby of a defunct high-tech firm in Seattle's Canyon Park, also home of the highest-tech giant, Microsoft. With those words the agent had already damned his sales pitch. The rest of the tour was merely a post-mortem. Why? Because of *feng shui* (pronounced "fung schway").

My client, a Chinese businessman holding a Ph. D. in a scientific field, was a shrewd purchaser of goods. In fact, he attended one or more used-goods auctions each week. You might surmise that he would have pursued a bargain lease opportunity with all the enthusiasm a born haggler could muster, but *feng shui* stopped him. It also stops hundreds of Asians daily who are potential lessors or purchasers of properties from concluding what looks like (to the uninitiated American salesman) a hot deal.

Feng shui literally means "wind, water" and is a life skill for knowing how the energies of wind and water circulate on earth. *Feng shui* is an ancient Chinese geomantic system used to determine the beneficial or harmful nature of land or buildings on the course of human life. *Feng shui* is living more harmoniously with the way of earth and heaven. There are the trained intuitive perceptions that a *feng shui xiansheng* (master geomancer) has about places. There are also thousands of rules of thumb that most Chinese use to judge the everyday fortune of homes and offices. Such *feng shui* knowledge is a pillar of Chinese culture.

My client had just applied the cardinal *feng shui* rule of thumb: always discover the history of the previous tenants. If their fortunes increased, so will the next occupant's. If their fortunes declined, however, so too will the next occupant's. An anthropologist, architect, or urban planner might consider such a judgment superstitious. If, for one moment, you see it from another perspective, this viewpoint is eminently scientific and empirical.

To the Chinese, a building and its decor are not things. They form a system that radiates an energy field. This field is referred to as *qi* (pronounced "chee") or basic life energy. Because you are a more conscious energy field than any building you may enter, you will recognize the energy field of the building, either as a fleeting sensation or a more intense aware-

The art of *feng shui* draws on the sciences of the heavens, the earth and the mind. It finds the most harmonious positions for people in rooms, for rooms in houses, and for houses in landscapes. *Feng shui* yokes the natural flow of energy from a place to a better human destiny.

ness. The longer you inhabit a building, the greater its effect on you will be. To my client, the egotistical president was nothing less than a dynamic experiment. His high-tech company in Suite 104D of the Cascade Building resulted in Chapter Eleven disaster. To the Western scientist, only repeatable experiments are verifiable. My Chinese client, however, was too shrewd to let his new biotechnology firm become a *feng shui* guinea pig, especially in the year of the horse. He knew this year ought to bring expansion and didn't want to risk a setback that would jeopardize the promise of the opportune moment.

How can you tell if a house or office, gravesite or campsite has good *feng shui?* The Chinese have developed four basic approaches. The first two, the landform and cosmological schools, are mentioned in most books on *feng shui*. The landform school surveys buildings and terrain existing in an area. Based on shapes and arrangements, the landform school draws inductive judgments about the nature of *qi* at that site and its probable effects on the family sponsoring the *feng shui* reading. For example, if a house has a non-rectangular shape like the letter "U," any activity that takes place in a room outside the rectangular part of the house will be outside household routine. The gourmet cook who moved into a Long Beach home with a dangling kitchen noticed his home cooking virtually stopped while his monthly restaurant expenditures increased significantly. The landform school is noted for locating and harnessing azure dragons, white tigers, red phoenixes and black turtles in the landscape. These poetic metaphors describe different types of vital energy emanating from the various mountains and valleys.

Another mode of *feng shui* thinking, the cosmological school, is famous for using a large compass called a *luo pan* that has from eight to thirty rings. The approach is to learn how a building site is oriented toward pre-existing energies in our solar system, and if possible to improve its correspondences to original nature. The site is checked for *yin-yang* balance, how it sits in relation to the 5 elements, 8 directions, 9 northern stars, 10 heavenly stems, 12 earthly branches, 24 solar fortnights, 28 lunar mansions, 64 hexagrams of the *I Ching*, or the 360 degrees of a circle. The cosmological *feng shui xian-sheng* seeks to place his patrons favorably in the mandala of heaven and earth.

The essence of cosmological *feng shui* is to organize your living so that it is like the natural order of the universe. Pay attention to details, including the direction your front door faces and the arrangement of the room where you receive guests. Effortless harmony with life is the result.

Not addressed in most popular books in English on *feng shui* are two remaining approaches: symbology and "feeling *qi*." Symbology looks for the meaning of objects and symbols with which people surround themselves. For instance, in a Seattle house, the kitchen was just off the living room. A sofa jutted out near the doorway to the kitchen, creating a thigh-high obstacle. The symbol said there was difficulty nurturing the family, physically and perhaps monetarily. The wife, an interior designer who did all the cooking, confided that she disliked cooking every meal and money had indeed become tight for them in the last half year. In the practice of *feng shui,* symbols are read in conjunction with information obtained in landform or cosmic surveys.

To some extent, if landforms, symbols or compass directions are interpreted, they say something secondary about what *qi* energy is doing. However, if you can feel *qi* itself, the strength, evenness and quality of flow, then you have a direct conduit of knowledge about influences to and from building and property. It is similar to taking a pulse in medical diagnosis — it is direct contact with the patient. In Chinese medicine, correctly assessing a person's *qi* reveals her or his state of health. In *feng shui,* correctly assessing a building or room's *qi* reveals how it will effect those living exterior and interior to it.

To have favorable *feng shui*, a place needs a dragon, guardians, water and a system to collect energy. A dragon in this context means a building should be backed up. Its rear and private section should have a feeling of security. Guardians, like the *Fu* dogs that flank Taoist temples and mandarin mansions, should provide a sense of protection right and left. Dragons and guardians can be buildings, hills, a stand of trees or even a single tree. Water refers to that which is basic to life: H_2O to plants, money to households, and plenty of walk-by or drive-by traffic to shops and marts. "Water" can be gauged in the amount of activity or *qi* around your place. The other requirements of good *feng shui* are useless if the energy flowing toward, around and by your front door can't be captured and a good portion of it used to nourish your family or business.

As for the realtor who earned no commission that day, my client and I took him to a Red Robin restaurant for locally brewed beer, lunch and a briefing on 3,000 years of *feng shui* principles. Our aim was to explain the basis by which Asian buyers judge the inner worth of property, so he could serve us more efficiently the next time and subsequently close more deals with Asians. For his part, he was glad to gain insight into why so many of his would-be deals with Asians had failed. It wasn't due to his salesmanship, but to a culture little known to him. Because he had years of experience in land and buildings and people's reactions to them, he felt many of the *feng shui* principles we presented were intuitively sensible, while some remained more arcane. Most importantly, he saw some particulars of Chinese culture rooted in the greater and universal relation of heaven, man and earth.

So what was wrong with the egotistical president's business area? Windows and wrong form! Windows are highly rated in contemporary American architecture for the views they offer and the natural light they provide. To the Chinese, windows also let *qi* out. The president's office was an irregular shape, like a fat piece of apple pie. All around the semicircular perimeter were windows while the president himself sat with his back to the only corner. A circular shape is *yang* — dynamic, creative and a spurt of energy, while a square or rectangle is *yin* — conserving, sustaining and enduring. At the *yang* area of the office all the company's creative energy flowed out the president's windows. Although the company had an innovative electronic product that produced good initial sales, expenses exceeded revenue from the very beginning. The gap continued to widen until bankruptcy court ended the imbalance. The presiding judge called it bad management. It was also fatal *feng shui*.

Chinese Philosophy

The poem quoted at left is from a work called the *Tao Te Ching*, also known as the *Lao Tzu*. The author, according to Chinese tradition, was *Lao Tzu*, which translated means "Old Master." *Lao Tzu* was said to be a contemporary of *Kung Fu Tzu* (Master *Kung Fu*), whom Westerners call Confucius. Modern scholars date *Lao Tzu* anywhere from 600 to 300 B.C. Some say many people authored the book over a period of centuries. Some also say it existed before the sixth century B.C., but only in oral tradition. However written, the poems are an important teaching. Every line can be interpreted on many levels, each reflecting the multifaceted Tao like a jewel reflects light.

The *Tao Te Ching* is the oldest work identified with the Chinese philosophy called Taoism. *Tao Te Ching* means "The Classic of the Way and Its Power." Tao refers to a path, or more figuratively, to a way of life that when followed leads to harmony with Nature. Within the Great Way of Tao, there are many smaller tao, such as *feng shui*, the tea ceremony and landscape painting. All teach how to tread a particular path about which you may have much native enthusiasm. The Great Tao is reflected and complete in each of the small ways. Each of the 81 poems in the *Tao Te Ching* gives instructions about how to recognize the Great Tao and follow it. No poem attempts to define what Tao is; rather, the poems merely hint.

A wheel? Thirty spokes
round a hub!
Yet, its empty hub makes
it useful.

A bowl? Clay spun on a
potter's wheel!
Yet, its empty hollow
makes it useful.

A house? Walls cut by
doors and windows!
Yet, its empty space
makes it useful.

So take gain from what is
here;
Draw its use from what's
not.

Tao Te Ching

- Lao Tzu

Vast emptiness, that's Tao!
Draw from it, you won't run out.
A fathomless abyss —
Maybe ancestor of all.
It smooths sharp edges;
Unravels hardened knots;
Tempers too harsh light;
Pervades this dusty world.
Deep in dark water, ever it seems clear:
I don't know from whom it comes,
But seems it was here before God.

Taoism has three branches in China: philosophy, mystical practice and religion. *Feng shui* has deep roots in Taoism, in all three of its schools. The poem at left applies to *feng shui* as much as it does to self-cultivation. Contemplate it carefully. Frank Lloyd Wright displayed part of this quotation in the auditorium of Taliesin, the architectural school he founded near Phoenix.

The meaning of emptiness and its uses are a deeply mystical pursuit in both Taoism and Buddhism. You will find if you study meditation, the arts of war, or if you play *Go* — a board game of strategy — that in order to master them, you have to master the art of the use of emptiness. All strategy relies on emptiness, sometimes sensed as open space, or perhaps as absence from a particular place. Emptiness is the essence of *ikebana* (flower arrangement) and also the essence of *feng shui*.

Don't confuse the Western connotations of emptiness with the Chinese meaning. Western emptiness implies a black void, a pathetic loneliness, a chaotic stretch of nothingness, and the numbing end of all existence. It brings to mind the works of Camus, Sarte, Kafka, and the expression of Nothing in Genesis. By contrast, the Chinese idea of *wu* (*mu* in Japanese) is of a mysterious and deep but vibrant potential that continually boils over in creation into beings and things. The beings and things that are created exist according to their natures, then return to *wu*. *Wu* is the nature of the Tao or the origin, support and aim of all. *Wu* is alive with energy, is intimate with all beings, and is the basis of life. Chaos comes not from *wu* but from the unbalancing of life forces. Everything makes sense once you understand *wu*.

The Zen Master *Chao-chou T'sung-shen* was asked whether only human beings have enlightened nature or whether all other beings do, too. A disciple specifically asked: "Does a dog have Buddha nature?" *Chao-chou* replied: "*Wu!*" The answer has several meanings. On a very literal level, *wu* means "no." *Wu* also sounds like how dogs express themselves. What *Chao-chou* also was pointing toward was that not only does all life partake of enlightened nature, but that enlightenment is of the clear nature of emptiness that runs through every thing and every being.

*Tao never does;
yet through it all things
are done.*

Tao Te Ching

Learning to recognize *wu* and then using it is the work of a lifetime. Understanding and applying emptiness as well as the other aspects of Taoist philosophy discussed here will make the practice of *feng shui* for you an art of subtlety. Chinese philosophy is considered validated only when you test it out in the practicality of the adventures of your own life. Understanding Taoist philosophy will not just add depth to your practice of *feng shui*, but as you use *feng shui,* you will discover you are living philosophy and art in your everyday life.

Yin and Yang

The most basic idea in Chinese philosophy, found in every one of its ancient arts and sciences, is *yin* and *yang*. *Yin* and *yang* arise after the One, then give birth to the 10,000 things — including the extent of the material universe. In order for a human being to pass through the stages of creation in reverse order to the source, *yin* and *yang* must be in a balanced condition. This is true even if your goal is less mystical. For example, to remove an obstruction to your happiness, regain a state of health, or create a more harmonious household, *yin* and *yang* must be in balance.

Originally *yang* meant "banners waving in the sun," while the meaning of *yin* was "cloudy, overcast." *Yin* and *yang* are the penultimate forces in the universe that do not directly show themselves on earth, but we can recognize the reflections of their characteristics and their manifestations.

Characteristics of *Yin* and *Yang*

1. *Yin* and *yang* always appear together, never without each other.
2. *Yin* and *yang* are in constant states of change and balance.
3. *Yin* and *yang* are not real, they are relative to each other.
4. At the height of *yin*, *yang* ascends and *yin* declines.
5. At the height of *yang*, *yin* ascends and *yang* declines.
6. *Yang* and *yin* appear as dynamic pairs of opposites.
7. *Yang* and *yin* compound each other, layer on layer.
8. *Yang* and *yin* create earthbound things in six stages.
9. Phenomena hide and play in the wake of *yang* and *yin*.

Enso

Tai Ji Tu

There are several ways to represent the evolution of the universe from the One, which is the primal symbol (called *enso* in Japanese), to the Two, represented by the *Tai Ji Tu,* commonly called the *yin/yang* symbol. The circle represents the Ultimate Source, half *yin* and half *yang*, each with the embryonic seed of the other growing within it. The S-shaped boundary between the two demonstrates that their borders are never fixed. Because of the constant flux of *yin* and *yang*, like waves in the sea, the primary attribute of Tao is change. The *Tai Ji Tu* shows the interaction of *yin* and *yang* and is meant to be a mandala for contemplation.

If you move too far, right or left, you get pulled off balance. That's our human condition. If you want to live wholeheartedly again, you have to learn to walk between the magnetic fields of *yin* and *yang*. That journey in Zen is called "passing through the gateless gate."

The ultimate force in the universe has no name, no description. It precedes time, space and Creation. All evolution rides on the crest of waves from the ultimate, materializing in the physical realm. Evolution toward the One, the ultimate, is through the gate of *yang* and *yin*.

The Manifestations of *Yang* and *Yin*

bright	dark
rising	sinking
moving	still
expansive	contractive
innovative	traditional
creative	receptive
expending	conserving
white	black
north pole	south pole
mountain	valley
straight road	meandering road
linear time	cyclic time
physical world	astral world
banners waving in the sun	cloudy and overcast

Below are the Chinese characters (*kanji*) for *yang* and *yin*. The part on the left side of both *kanji*, called a radical, is a picture of a district. The right side of the *kanji* for *yang* shows the district of the sun and its rays; the *kanji* for *yin* shows the district of shadow.

yang   *yin*

The *I Ching,* Book of Changes

Change

The *I Ching,* translated variously as the *Book of Changes* or the *Classic of Change,* is perhaps the oldest writing on philosophy, cosmology, divination and self-transformation in Chinese civilization. It is one of very few books consistently to have escaped intentional destruction by despots from the first *Chin* emperor (221 B.C.) to Mao Zedong of our era. Therefore, the *I Ching* must be essential to Chinese culture or offer some irresistible advantage to sages and dictators alike. Although later books discuss *feng shui* as an independent intuitive science and art, the tap root is from the *I Ching.* It reveals the pattern and pulse of life.

One approach to the wisdom of the *I Ching* is to contemplate each of the 64 images that show some natural phenomena as a pattern of change. By contemplating the image or basic pattern of *feng shui* found in the *I Ching,* you will widen your circle of understanding of *feng shui* and the world in which you live. Then *feng shui* will make sense as an inner and more intimate truth.

Each image in the *I Ching* is composed of six lines, broken (*yin*) and unbroken *(yang).* Six combinations of *yin* and *yang* make up all 64 images, called *gua,* shown in the *I Ching.* Three-line combinations of *yin* and *yang* represent the eight forces in the phenomenal world, which are illustrated in the River Lo Map on page 49. Two of the eight forces are wind and water, which appear in only two of the *gua:* #48, the Well *(Jing)* and #59, Dispersion *(Huan).* Below is the image of the Well, which is closely connected to *feng shui.*

The Well

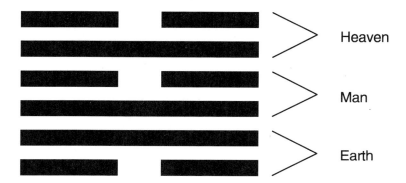

Well

The Well

The town may be changed,
But the well cannot be changed.
It neither decreases nor increases.
They come and go and draw from the well.
If one gets down almost to the water
And the rope does not go all the way
Or the jug breaks, it brings misfortune.

                                  - translated by R. Wilhelm and C. Baynes

In the *gua* of the Well, the *I Ching* reveals two things: the first is that *feng shui* is not of the order of unchanging life forces. Rather, it is an unchanging method for drawing temporal and primordial sustenance out of the deep, dark, mysterious ground of life. The second is to be thorough in your education about how to use *feng shui,* for if your learning is too shallow (rope too short) or you are careless in what you learn (jug breaks), you will suffer the misfortune of mistaken use. In other words, if you organize your house, office or property using mistaken notions about what you think *feng shui* to be, the mistakes you make will further separate you from harmony with nature. The cure is to be thorough, to continue to nourish yourself deeply from the Well. Then your use of *feng shui* will be as the *I Ching* indicates:

One draws from the well
Without hindrance.
It is dependable.
Supreme good fortune.

The *kanji* for the Well looks like a tic-tac-toe grid and forms the basis for the River Lo Map. It shows a basic rural organization of eight land parcels around a central parcel containing the common well, and can be seen as a rudimentary urban-rural land use plan and basic community structure.

Wu Xing: The Five Agents

Wood

Fire

Earth

Metal

Water

Similar to the concept of the four elements in Greek philosophy with a fifth element being aether or space, the Chinese have the idea of the five agents *(wu xing)*. The *kanji* for "agent" literally means "to go." To the Greeks, the elements were building blocks of substance, but to the Chinese, the five agents are dynamic processes or energies of nature. The *wu xing* are: wood, fire, earth, metal and water. They occur in several patterns. One is the order of mutual promotion or mutual arising. In the diagram below, follow the agents in a clockwise direction. Another pattern is the order of mutual control or mutual destruction. In the diagram, follow the internal arrows in the star in a clockwise direction.

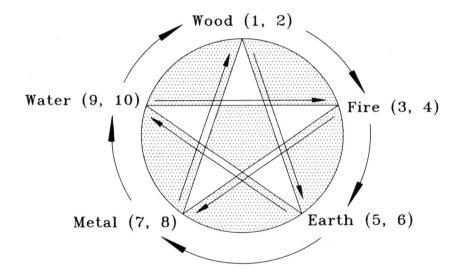

Each of the *wu xing* agents corresponds to many phenomena as do each of the eight trigrams of the *I Ching.* For instance, because spring is associated with wood, when it is spring, wood is prominent and active. Correspondences include seasons, times of day, directions, colors, body organs, acupuncture meridians, types of tastes, planets, days of the week, shapes, etc. When you observe one of more of the correspondences in a property, house, office or room, indirectly you are perceiving the reflection of that energy there. Diagnoses and cures in *feng shui,* as much as in acupuncture and herbal medicine, rely on accurately assessing the strength and balance of *wu xing.* A table of correspondences appears on the next page.

Correspondences of the Five Agents (*Wu Xing*)

Category	Wood	Fire	Earth	Metal	Water
Zang organ	Liver	Heart	Spleen	Lung	Kidney
Fu organ	Gall bladder	Small intestine	Stomach	Large intestine	Urinary bladder
Sense organ	Eye	Tongue	Mouth	Nose	Ear
Body tissue	Tendon	Vessel	Muscle	Skin and Hair	Bone
Emotions	Kindness and Anger	Joy and Hate	Calm and Worry	Courage and Grief	Gentility and Fear
Season	Spring	Summer	Indian summer	Autumn	Winter
Environment	Wind	Heat	Damp	Dryness	Cold
Growth stage	Germination	Growth	Transformation	Reaping	Storing
Color	Green	Red	Yellow	White	Black or Blue
Taste	Sour	Bitter	Sweet	Spicy hot	Salty
Direction	East	South	Middle	West	North
Room	Kitchen	Living	Dining	Bedroom	Bath
Planet	Jupiter	Mars	Saturn	Venus	Mercury
Chinese Character (*Kanji*)	木	火	土	金	水

The Twelve Chinese Zodiac Signs
The Twelve Earthly Branches

Chinese astrology, called *ming shu,* is unique among astrological systems. It uses the familiar ten-and-twelve system like other astrologies, but the basic time frame for humans is a twelve-year period that forms five repetitions to make a sixty-year cycle of life. There was also a yearly solar calendar, linked to a lunar almanac showing which of the thirty-six human activities in a rural society were favored or maligned each day. The Chinese not only employed the zodiac constellations around the equator, but also had a separate astrological system based on the constellations centering around the North Pole stars. The interaction of all these systems was complex, and much of the connections among these Chinese systems of time and space are now lost knowledge of a wiser antiquity. Since astrology relates as much to movement in space as it does to the passage of time, Chinese astrology formed one leg of practice of *feng shui.*

Chinese astrology tries to account for the motions of the earth and the heavens practically and philosophically. When to plant and harvest is one set of concerns. The arrangement and goal of the universe is another equally important line of inquiry. If astrology can establish what the order of heaven and earth is, then we as human beings can locate where our place is in that scheme in an ultimate sense, and form a *feng shui* perspective in an everyday sense. Harmony with the universe, ultimately and moment by moment, is what *ming shu* and *feng shui* are both about. If a person can so structure his or her life that it is in direct imitation to the order of the universe, then he or she cannot help but be in harmony. Good fortune is the beneficial result of being in harmony and moving as one with heaven and earth. The specifics of knowing which action to take, where and when involve interpreting the signs of heaven. Although the following will not explain how to apply astrological knowledge in *feng shui,* it will introduce you to the flavor of the signs and their meanings.

The Chinese Zodiac

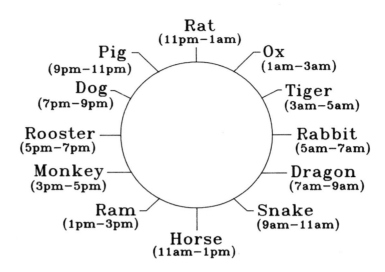

The Chinese zodiac, like the familiar one the West inherited from the ancient Sumerians, has twelve signs. Made famous by Chinese restaurant place-mats, the Chinese zodiac is linked primarily to a twelve-year cycle, but also corresponds to time measured in double hours (see above) and to the directions of the compass (see the diagrams on the next page). In East Asia a day cycle was measured in twelve equal units, each named after an animal. For example, the hour of the tiger, as measured on a Swiss watch, was 120 minutes, from 3:00 a.m. to 5:00 a.m., a double hour. The animal hours measure cycles of subtle changes of energy on earth. The Chinese zodiac, or "The Twelve Earthly Branches" as its more basic cyclic series is called, is used in the cosmological school of *feng shui* and is consulted as part of the *luo pan*, the *feng shui* compass.

The original names and meanings of the twelve branches, as well as their later correspondences with the twelve animals, follow:

I.	*Tzu*	Child, son	Rat	VII.	*Wu*	Noon	Horse
II.	*Ch'ou*	Clown	Ox	VIII.	*Wei*	Not yet	Ram
III.	*Yin*	Reverence	Tiger	IX.	*Shen*	Stretch	Monkey
IV.	*Mao*	Pleiades	Rabbit	X.	*Yu*	Liquor	Rooster
V.	*Ch'en*	Dawn, eclipse	Dragon	XI.	*Shu*	Weapon	Dog
VI.	*Ssu*	Snake	Snake	XII.	*Hai*	Darkness	Pig

Compass Direction and the Twelve Branches

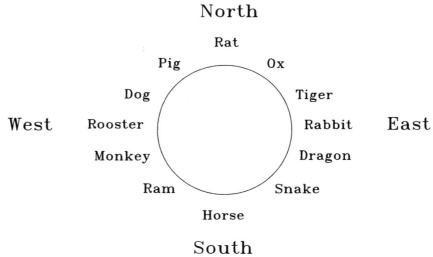

The illustrations below show how the signs for the various Chinese zodiac years are compatible or incompatible with one another, as represented by the interior linking lines indicating the relationship.

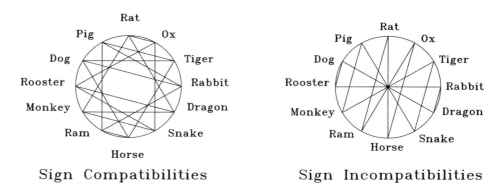

Sign Compatibilities   Sign Incompatibilities

On the following page, the five agents *(wu xing)* are linked with the twelve earthly branches to form the sixty-year cycle. The most recent cycle started in 1984, or the Chinese year 4683 since the Yellow Emperor *(Huang Ti)* ruled. One use of the sixty-year table is to discover your yearly agent and animal so that you know what kind of energy you have. The table can also tell you which directions and what times of day and season are favorable, difficult or neutral for you. Then, in *feng shui*, you adjust the energies of place to harmonize with your personal energy.

Five Agents and Twelve Animals
Cycle of Years: 1901 - 2000 (4599 - 4698)

19 Feb 1901 **Metal Ox**	8 Feb 1921 **Metal Rooster**	27 Jan 1941 **Metal Snake**	15 Feb 1961 **Metal Ox**	5 Feb 1981 **Metal Rooster**
8 Feb 1902 **Water Tiger**	28 Jan 1922 **Water Dog**	15 Feb 1942 **Water Horse**	5 Feb 1962 **Water Tiger**	25 Jan 1982 **Water Dog**
29 Jan 1903 **Water Hare**	16 Feb 1923 **Water Pig**	5 Feb 1943 **Water Sheep**	25 Jan 1963 **Water Hare**	13 Feb 1983 **Water Pig**
16 Feb 1904 **Wood Dragon**	5 Feb 1924 **Wood Rat**	25 Jan 1944 **Wood Monkey**	13 Feb 1964 **Wood Dragon**	2 Feb 1984 **Wood Rat**
4 Feb 1905 **Wood Snake**	25 Jan 1925 **Wood Ox**	13 Feb 1945 **Wood Rooster**	2 Feb 1965 **Wood Snake**	20 Feb 1985 **Wood Ox**
25 Jan 1906 **Fire Horse**	13 Feb 1926 **Fire Tiger**	2 Feb 1946 **Fire Dog**	21 Jan 1966 **Fire Horse**	9 Feb 1986 **Fire Tiger**
13 Feb 1907 **Fire Sheep**	2 Feb 1927 **Fire Hare**	22 Jan 1947 **Fire Pig**	9 Feb 1967 **Fire Sheep**	29 Jan 1987 **Fire Hare**
2 Feb 1908 **Earth Monkey**	23 Jan 1928 **Earth Dragon**	10 Feb 1948 **Earth Rat**	30 Jan 1968 **Earth Monkey**	17 Feb 1988 **Earth Dragon**
22 Jan 1909 **Earth Rooster**	10 Feb 1929 **Earth Snake**	29 Jan 1949 **Earth Ox**	17 Feb 1969 **Earth Rooster**	6 Feb 1989 **Earth Snake**
10 Feb 1910 **Metal Dog**	30 Jan 1930 **Metal Horse**	17 Feb 1950 **Metal Tiger**	6 Feb 1970 **Metal Dog**	27 Jan 1990 **Metal Horse**
30 Jan 1911 **Metal Pig**	17 Feb 1931 **Metal Sheep**	6 Feb 1951 **Metal Hare**	27 Jan 1971 **Metal Pig**	15 Feb 1991 **Metal Sheep**
18 Feb 1912 **Water Rat**	6 Feb 1932 **Water Monkey**	27 Jan 1952 **Water Dragon**	15 Feb 1972 **Water Rat**	4 Feb 1992 **Water Monkey**
6 Feb 1913 **Water Ox**	26 Jan 1933 **Water Rooster**	14 Feb 1953 **Water Snake**	3 Feb 1973 **Water Ox**	23 Jan 1993 **Water Rooster**
26 Jan 1914 **Wood Tiger**	14 Feb 1934 **Wood Dog**	3 Feb 1954 **Wood Horse**	23 Jan 1974 **Wood Tiger**	10 Feb 1994 **Wood Dog**
14 Feb 1915 **Wood Hare**	4 Feb 1935 **Wood Pig**	24 Jan 1955 **Wood Sheep**	11 Feb 1975 **Wood Hare**	31 Jan 1995 **Wood Pig**
3 Feb 1916 **Fire Dragon**	24 Jan 1936 **Fire Rat**	12 Feb 1956 **Fire Monkey**	31 Jan 1976 **Fire Dragon**	19 Feb 1996 **Fire Rat**
23 Jan 1917 **Fire Snake**	11 Feb 1937 **Fire Ox**	31 Jan 1957 **Fire Rooster**	18 Feb 1977 **Fire Snake**	7 Feb 1997 **Fire Ox**
11 Feb 1918 **Earth Horse**	31 Jan 1938 **Earth Tiger**	18 Feb 1958 **Earth Dog**	7 Feb 1978 **Earth Horse**	28 Jan 1998 **Earth Tiger**
1 Feb 1919 **Earth Sheep**	19 Feb 1939 **Earth Hare**	8 Feb 1959 **Earth Pig**	28 Jan 1979 **Earth Sheep**	16 Feb 1999 **Earth Hare**
20 Feb 1920 **Metal Monkey**	8 Feb 1940 **Metal Dragon**	28 Jan 1960 **Metal Rat**	16 Feb 1980 **Metal Monkey**	5 Feb 2000 **Metal Dragon**

Approaches to *Feng Shui*

In exploring the practice of *feng shui*, the questions why it is done, how it is done and how well is it done are important inquiries. Knowing the motivations, methods and levels of expertise reveal what the art of *feng shui* is actually about, and why it has continued to be practiced these many millennia. Knowing these will make you more comfortable and more confident so you can play with the art more freely, exploring its limits and potentials for yourself.

Folk *feng shui*

In China, much *feng shui* wisdom is embedded in the language and culture. This is so true that if you question someone from a rural village or a city neighborhood about the philosophy of *feng shui,* its theoretical under-pinnings or its alternate applications, most often you would be met by a blank stare. If, however, you asked what was the reason for the poor business of the herbal pharmacy at the end of the street, you would receive some answers that are of the realm of *feng shui* sprinkled among other commercial speculations. This is the tradition of folk *feng shui,* tested and handed down in oral tradition and experience for forty or more centuries. Some Chinese people practice the tradition mixed with misinformation, whereas others will test and refine the tradition further for practical use in their daily living. Because I call it folk *feng shui,* I do not intend to dimin-ish it. In fact, Chinese who practice folk *feng shui* as an extension of their cultural awareness and learning can be quite skilled practitioners of the art. Personal and cultural harmony is the motive for folk *feng shui.*

Chinese Lotus Charm paper cut folk design

Folk *feng shui* knowledge is not uniform throughout Asia, or even through parts of the same region. Each Asian family has its own tradition of what it considers good *feng shui* in real estate. To the Western realtor, architect or interior designer, the task in satisfying Asian clients is to first find out the specifics of what the client considers good *feng shui.* For example, one Chinese client may want only a south-facing front door, while another will consider an east-facing bedroom the most important quality. A Korean client may rule out a home with more than three steps up, while a Japanese client may not even consider a corner lot for home or business. Folk *feng shui* has many versions with differing priorities, so it takes pa-tience and insight for an American to learn them and prosper.

Power *feng shui*

Whenever *feng shui* is applied to make things better in life, a person would realize that he or she is gaining an advantage. Applied to competition, that edge might lead more easily to economic or political dominance. In short, some Chinese use *feng shui* for the express purpose of gaining power for themselves or their masters. This is power *feng shui*. Hong Kong banks and big businesses spend millions to get a *feng shui* advantage that translates into competitive control. Of course, the savvy competitor will reply in kind, leading to *feng shui* warfare.

There is a considerable tradition for the practice of power *feng shui*. Many ancient military strategies, including *Sun Tzu,* address how to seize the winning advantage by any means, including shrewd use of *feng shui*. The strategic use of space, ranging from the games of *Go* and *Shogi* to military campaigns, is an extension of *feng shui*. Historically, Chinese imperial governments have used *feng shui* to plan public works and monuments. Gain, not harmony, is the motive of power *feng shui*.

The tallest and greatest buildings of the modern era on every continent are not fortresses, churches or state buildings as in other eras, but commercial structures housing corporate headquarters. A quick scan of the skyline of any major world city will show that commercial buildings are tallest, reflecting the highest status held in their respective societies, whether in Chicago, Tokyo, Hong Kong, Singapore, Sydney, London or Cairo. It should not be surprising that of all the reasons for employing *feng shui*, power *feng shui* is the most popular motivation.

When Chinese companies open plants or offices in Europe or North America, they will employ local architects and contractors, but also will bring in their own practitioners of power *feng shui* to nail down that competitive advantage. You can be certain that the successful Asian corporations that invest millions of dollars in *feng shui* consultation fees — and the resulting landscape and building changes — are acting strictly as businessmen calculating return on investment. They know the value of their *feng shui* investment to the sixth decimal place. If there is any proof required that *feng shui* works, the vast amounts of commercial and military investment in *feng shui* should furnish that proof by monetary proxy.

Feng Shui Tao

The *kanji* for Tao (*Do,* in Japanese) pictures a road and more broadly means "a Way." Many of the arts, sciences and crafts of the East were originally taught as a Tao, meaning that a person studied a subject not only to become expert at a particular set of skills, but primarily as a method of self-cultivation. You may be familiar with the arts of *Chado* (The Way of Tea), *Bushido* (The Way of the Warrior), *Aikido* (The Way of Harmonious Energy), and *Zendo* (The Way of Meditation). *Feng shui* also is practiced as a Tao. It is the Way of Wind and Water. Concentrating on how landscapes and buildings effect human and sentient life, the practitioner of *Feng Shui Tao* continually seeks to arrange spaces and places in ever greater harmony with nature. The nature with which *Feng Shui Tao* seeks greater harmony is both Mother Nature (or Gaia in the Western sense) and Primordial Nature, which is the ground of life before Creation. The motivation of *Feng Shui Tao* is self-cultivation and self-realization. *Feng Shui Tao* is the perspective encouraged in this book.

Tao

Although the three basic varieties of *feng shui* practice are described above, you may find each of them mixed with the other, or with rituals from Taoism as a religion or a mystical practice. The Chinese are remarkably open about religion and philosophy and do not expect a person to be either Taoist or Confucian, Buddhist or Christian. As a result, you will find Buddhist, Christian and Confucian varieties of *feng shui* as well. The *feng shui* blend is not judged by some standard of doctrinal purity, but rather by intent and result. In other words, how well does your individual practice of *feng shui* accomplish what you expect? That is the more accurate standard of practical *feng shui* ability.

As with all other human pursuits, there are true masters of *feng shui* who may or may not carry the title *Feng Shui Xiansheng* or Master Geomancer. There are amateurs and professionals. There are *feng shui* practitioners from the spectra of social class and education. There are those who are very accomplished, those who are quite competent, those who are barely able, those who are learning, those who are misguided, and those who are charlatans. In ancient China, many scholars who did not receive appointments to government office went into the practice of *feng shui.* Like practitioners of other arts and professions, you have to look past the wrappings to find the value you need.

When it comes to performing the art of *feng shui,* there are four practice approaches. The landform and cosmological approaches are considered the two main schools, incorporating the *qi* and symbolism approaches within.

The Landform School

This approach concentrates on how the shapes of geological formations as well as the shapes of artificial landscapes such as streets, neighborhoods and cities affect buildings. On a smaller level, the shapes of buildings, rooms and furniture also are subjects of the landform approach. This school seeks to note, directly or by correspondence, the nature of the energy field emanating from a site and to inductively reason what the effects will be on the inhabitants. Changes are made to conform and harmonize with the form systems present.

The most basic shapes in two dimensions are the triangle, square and circle, which in three dimensions become the pyramid, cube and sphere. To the Chinese, a form has an energy dimension as well as a shape dimension. A lot of scientific and occult study has gone into the special forces that emanate not only from the Great Pyramid at Giza, but from any similar pyramid oriented in precise north-south alignment. The philosophy of the *feng shui* landform school maintains that every shape emanates a force field. In fact, every line, whether a clothesline, electrical line, or the edge of a roof, has the power to retard or accelerate *qi* energy. By studying the effect of these shapes and managing their expressions, you can learn to improve or unbalance the energy field of a building and ultimately the people who work or live there.

Of the basic shapes, the most difficult to work with is the triangle. The obvious reason is that it is hard to place furniture or make efficient use of the space in angles less than 90°. Another reason is that a triangle points a sharp edge at another building or the people entering it. That edge carries hard *qi* that has an attacking quality. Triangles, though great in war and business, are disaster when used in a house or a church. Squares or rectangles are considered *yin* shapes that conserve and hold energy. For instance, a table that is square will hold a meeting longer than any other shape. It will also hold a discussion over dinner longer, or a detail-oriented session to hash out a full contract. By contrast, a circle is *yang* in nature and spins energy away. While great for generating creative ideas, a semicircular seating arrangement, whether in a hotel or a living room, will not hold guests very long. In fact, the very shape speeds them on their way.

The landform school recognizes the energy of hills and mountains and gives them picturesque names, like azure dragon, white tiger, red phoenix, or black tortoise. As the English poet William Wordsworth said, the earth itself is alive with energy, not only the plants and animals upon it. That energy comes in varieties, which correspond to *yin* and *yang,* to the five agents *(wu xing)* or to the eight small trigrams *(gua)* of the *I Ching.* By knowing the preponderance of energy in the land, a business owner can make adjustments in the shapes of rooms and furniture to augment or to counterbalance the intensity of the energies already present there.

The Cosmological School

This approach to *feng shui* seeks to discover in what relation to the primordial universe a building or landform places a human being. The method is to use a *luo pan,* or *feng shui* compass, to measure the directions and correspondences with the heavens that exist at a place. Through proper orientation, the building or furniture in a room can be arranged in the same manner as the heavens in divine imitation. Being placed in the favorable mandala of original nature, a human cannot fail to achieve his or her heart's content, including the supreme realization of the enlightened mind.

Effective use of the cosmological approach requires an in-depth understanding of how heaven and earth came to be, what are their natures, and what are their ends. This is a question of philosophy. To understand and effectively use the cosmological school of *feng shui,* you need to learn Chinese philosophy, especially the *yin/yang* school. The *yin/yang* school addresses itself to climatology, agriculture, astrology, health and other practical sciences. You also need to engage frequently in contemplation of this wondrous universe in which we live.

Much of the subject matter for this study of philosophy can be found in the great classics of Chinese literature, the *Tao Te Ching* and the *I Ching,* which are described in greater detail in the section on Chinese philosophy. Because the cosmological approach is the most cryptic and mysterious of the four approaches, it is often misunderstood by Westerners. Patient study and reflection will make *feng shui* rules for the ordering of buildings more comprehensible and sensible and seem less like superstition.

The easiest cosmological school concept is that directions have great effect on the energy a building draws to itself and its inhabitants. Commercial success and fame are best drawn in by a south door; the unfolding of your deepest destiny by a north door; involvement with family and community by an east door; and, children, joy and students by a west door. (Please see the River Lo Map on page 49 for a more detailed presentation.) First a word of orientation: when standing looking out your front door, the direction you are facing is your door's direction and influence.

The Symbolic School

This approach to *feng shui* assesses the meaning of the symbols with which people or families consciously, or more often unconsciously, surround themselves. This approach also assesses symbols in and around adjoining properties that the family did not place, but that nonetheless reveal what harmonious and inharmonious influences are being attracted. Recommended cures involve replacing inharmonious and unconscious symbols with positive ones. This approach also enjoins employment of ritual to resolve life problems.

Symbols are universal, social and personal. Symbols also have meanings on multiple levels at the same time. Although accurately interpreting symbols is difficult, it can be revealing. Not to examine the symbols and meanings of the artwork above your fireplace is the same as ignoring the self-knowledge revealed every night in your dreams. The idea is simple. Every symbol with which you physically surround yourself at home or at the office is being activated every time you, a family member, co-worker, or visitor enters a room. After a number of activation encounters with any symbol, it reaches a threshold of precipitation, and enters your life on the emotional or physical levels. This approach to *feng shui* asks you if the symbols you are displaying are what you really want to activate in your life.

Poetry, art and dance are full of symbols, but so is your daily behavior, no matter how mundane it may seem. We think of them as routines or habits, but every act we perform is a ritual. Some are liberating, some bring joy, and some bring only dullness or alienation to the spirit. The symbolic approach to *feng shui* evaluates your daily routines. It takes into account behaviors that you would like to change. You could say that it attempts to program your mind consciously and positively so you can achieve your aspirations more readily.

An example is a shaky relationship. After seeing counselors or reflecting on the state of a marriage or friendship, each party knows what he or she ought to do to make things work. But even with that knowledge, they may still find it difficult to dissolve the obstructions causing their disharmony. A ritual such as meditating together, a tea ceremony, or even an evening walk away from family concerns, with conscious repetition, can dissolve the obstructions when rationality cannot. The symbolic approach to *feng shui* replaces destructive symbols with positive ones and alienating behavior with harmonizing rituals. Either way, this branch of *feng shui* seeks to cure human beings where they are at a deep level, transforming blinding emotion into intuition, confusion into insight, and dissatisfaction into joyful clarity.

The *Qi* School

This approach to *feng shui* seeks to sense *qi* fields directly, both of the occupants and the site, and to ascertain their harmony or disharmony. In modern times this may also include the measurement of unseen rays and waves such as electrical, cathode, VLF, ELF, microwave, etc. and may require insulating the inhabitants against harmful levels. Perceiving the *qi* of a place is a more direct connection to a site than the other approaches. Cures may take the form of intervention directly at the *qi* level as well as any one of the cures employed in the other schools. The wise *feng shui* scholar will integrate all approaches.

Qi: Life Energy

What is *qi*?

Qi (pronounced "chee," also written sometimes as *ch'i*) is basic life energy. The *kanji* for *qi* is made up of two parts, as shown below. The top section is the image of steam or clouds rising, while the lower part is a rice grain. The idea expressed in the *kanji* of *qi* is that of a subtle but sensible force that provides nourishment. The phenomenon of *qi* has been described as bioplasmic energy, the life-field or the L-field by various contemporary researchers. Other ancient cultures have called it *ki* (Japanese), *lung* (Tibetan) and *prana* (Sanskrit) and have referred to it in their arts and sciences. *Qi* can be conceived as a force that is subtler than physical matter, the motion of which precedes and mediates change in physical matter by its change of flow or intensity.

Qi

This may sound nonscientific as a definition. The Western scientific bias is that if a phenomenon cannot be measured and quantified with existing instruments, then the phenomenon is unproven, and so does not exist. It is possible, however, for people to verify for themselves that *qi* exists. It is also evident that the cultivation of *qi* is central to development and superior accomplishment in the Ways. For instance, diagnosis and treatment in acupuncture and Chinese herbology depend on discovering, assessing, then redirecting a patient's *qi* to effect cures from diseases. Since Chinese medicine has survived perhaps fifty centuries of empirical testing, there is verity that *qi* is a force. Regard well what a recent Tokyo subway ad said: *"Ki ga aru!" Qi* exists!

How is *qi* used?

In *Shodo,* the Way of Calligraphy, after students are taught how to brush *kanji,* how to mix ink and how to select paper, they are taught how to write with *qi.* The calligrapher directs *qi* through arm, hand, brush, ink and paper to form the message. Calligraphy is judged by how alive *kanji* are. This is true also of *sumi-e* painting. The liveliness comes from linking art and *qi* in indissoluble union. In the martial arts, the practitioner with the greatest force of *qi* is the one who is never thrown. In all the Ways, there is the same training, and in *Feng Shui Tao,* it is no different. We learn to sense, direct and surrender to the art of *feng shui* through *qi.*

A *qi* experience   There are many exercises for experiencing *qi*. A very simple one is to rub your palms together vigorously for perhaps fifteen seconds. As soon as you finish, place your hands six to ten inches apart, palm facing palm. Hold your hands at the level of your navel, and six to ten inches away from your body. Relax! You will feel a slightly magnetic pull of one palm toward the other. If you have difficulty feeling this, slowly move your palms closer together until you do feel it. Play with that faint magnetic feeling for a while, first compressing it slightly, then pulling away some. As you play with the magnetic feeling, the flow of *qi* will increase and become easier to sense. *"Ki ga aru!"*

Qi gong, a method for self-cultivation

In China, the method for cultivating *qi* is called *qi gong* (pronounced "chee goong"). Sometimes it is written in Roman letters *(romaji)* as *chi gung* or *chi kung.*

Qi, or life energy, infuses everything on planet earth, from a quartz crystal to a human being. *Qi* is an energy force long recognized not only in China, but in Japan, Korea, India, Indochina and Tibet as finer and more subtle than electric, magnetic or thermonuclear energies. In China, *qi* has been recognized as the subtle bridge from the physical to the emotional to the mental and beyond. The most visible root of *qi* is in breathing, yet its influence is not confined to the lungs or circulatory system, but suffuses every atom and subatomic particle of living matter. To the ancients, all matter is animated by and radiates life force.

Qi gong means "*qi* accomplishment." Because the Chinese language is so compact, a more ready English rendering is "the result of releasing, accumulating, moving, using and transforming life energy." Though it may sound complicated, correct *qi gong* practice requires relaxation, perseverance and a sense of play. Of the three requirements, the most difficult is perseverance, but none of the foundations of *qi gong* practice is beyond a person possessed of even underaverage abilities. If you approach *qi gong* with a sense of playful exploration, then even perseverance is more easily attained.

Qi gong refers to one of more than 6,000 sets of practices, sometimes referred to as "internal exercises," that are used to increase the amount and flow of qi available to a person. There are Buddhist, Taoist and Confucian types of qi gong. There are qi gong practices directed at restoring health in general or directed toward curing diseases of particular organ systems. There are qi gong practices devised to increase abilities in the martial arts, in the arts of painting and calligraphy, for psychic development, or for meditation. There are numerous qi gong practices for each of the Ways.

Some qi gong systems concentrate on the achievement of specific feats like the cure of weak kidneys, the ability to hurl a lance through a board, the ninja-like ability to become invisible, the capacity in landscape painting to continue to move ink after it has been applied to the paper, or even the ability to make clouds rain. There are systems of qi gong specifically designed to prolong a lifetime to at least 100 years and to as many as 150 years, while others strive for nothing less than attainment of immortality like the nine ancient Taoist sages.

If you observe other people performing qi gong, it appears as if they are doing exercises that sometimes look like Indian yoga, sometimes like breathing sequences or sometimes like forms from the Chinese martial arts of Tai Chi Chuan or Kung Fu. Just sitting, standing or walking can be the outward appearance of a qi gong practice, but something else is happening inside. Some qi gong movements are exercises that can be done alone, while others are part of a sequence that must be performed together to be effective. Since qi gong can take so many forms, including wake up exercises, it is hard to generalize about what it looks like. It is easy to recognize if you practice even a little.

As you practice qi gong, you will become increasingly sensitive to the energies of other persons and of place. More directly, you will be able to sense and understand the qi fields of landscapes, buildings, families and companies. Naturally, your insight and ability to improve the feng shui of almost any place will markedly expand as you continue to practice qi gong. Once you become focused on controlling and balancing your energy, your sense of the energy around you will be heightened. Remember, the paths to relaxation, to health, to increased vitality, to increased intelligence, to greater artistic perception and expression, to extraordinary accomplishment, to self-actualization and to the highest enlightenment are all along the same way.

Qi gong practices are usually named with a poetic metaphor such as standing crane, eight treasures or empty hand styles. A few exercises from spinning dragon *qi gong* are better taught in person at the workshop. The practice is not directed toward a particular end and is sometimes referred to as "body and mind drop off." This means that the ultimate goal of spinning dragon *qi gong* is the same as Zen meditation or *zazen*. The aim is to allow the small, grasping, unhappy and never-satisfied self to lose its edges of pride, distraction and discontent. Of themselves, greater health and vitality, peace of mind, and vastness of spirit will appear from behind the clouds of the small self dissolved by the practice of spinning dragon *qi gong* and *zazen*.

Spinning Dragon

Qi gong is not so hard to find. In China, it is everywhere, especially in the parks at daybreak. In America, if you are not a martial arts student, you are most likely to encounter *qi gong* when you visit a practitioner of acupuncture or Chinese herbal medicine. Often *qi gong* exercises are prescribed to help a patient overcome an ill health condition or to increase overall vitality so the body can cure itself with greater ease and speed in complement with acupuncture, massage, dietary or herbal treatments. All too often *qi gong* is prescribed when nothing else works. Even as a last resort in healing, *qi gong* is remarkable. In China there are clinics whose sole treatment regime is teaching patients how to manage pain, or partially or completely heal themselves through the practice of *qi gong*.

What is "Good" *Feng Shui?*

Harmony

It is much easier to point out inharmonious arrangements of sites, homes and buildings — what is called "bad" *feng shui.* That is because each person entered this world with a weight of *karma* that caused imbalance. Naturally, places reflect the imbalance each of us is attempting to absolve from our lives. What is called "good" *feng shui* is a gracious and harmonious arrangement of the more important aspects of our lives. A human being with unlimited "good" *feng shui* has no necessity to be earthbound and live in a home — he or she lives freely and confidently at home anywhere in the vast universe.

Improving the *feng shui* of a house or workplace will improve the quality and satisfaction of your life in a positive way. The hallmarks of "good" *feng shui,* which relate to the five agents *(wu xing)* and beyond, are discussed below. These hallmarks are not absolute things a house or office has. Rather, they are qualities about a site or building arrayed in balance. They can be present in the exterior or interior, and can be applied to any level: the property as a whole, a room, a yard or a corner. This means it is possible to have "good" *feng shui* in one room and "bad" *feng shui* in another.

Earth Dragon

To have an earth dragon in this context means that your house has mighty backing. In nature it means that a great hill, mountain or stand of trees taller than the building serves as backdrop. In a city, it may mean that a taller building to the rear serves as backing. The earth dragon is a foundation and must be kept at a proportional distance behind. To be effective, the earth dragon should be directly behind your building in line with the front door, and should be tall enough to be seen when you are standing at a distance from the building roughly equal to its height. If it is too far away or off to one side, its power will not be felt. If it is too close, its power will not support the building, but will overpower both building and occupants within. The earth dragon is powerful and must be respected, yet its power should be put to benevolent use.

Wood Guardians

Flanking any building should be the protectors, lending support right and left. In nature these guardians could be smaller hills, trees or bushes proportionally sized and spaced. In a city, guardians may be the buildings to the immediate right and left. Guardians offer both protection from enemies and positive support. The best guardians are alive and organic, and may include your next door neighbors and their condo. Guardians may also be symbolic like the *Fu* dogs that flank the main entrances of some Chinese buildings. Symbolic guardians, nonetheless, represent living, protective beings from myth or the worlds beyond such as elementals, sprites, animal spirits, immortals, deities, sages and *bodhisattvas*.

Water Course

Water means actual water, but it also means any and all energy types that flow and circulate near, around or through a site. These energies, including *qi,* usually flow in a pathway and are meant to bathe and nourish a site. Any energy river in this context is a water course and all water courses bring opportunity. Nurturing energy for the goals of the building inhabitants is by definition a "good" water course. To trees and plants, a "good" water course brings enough H_2O to sustain growth, but not to overwhelm. To an haute boutique, a "good" water course brings enough well-to-do shoppers past the front door. To a rural office, it brings electricity and phones to operate a distant, profitable business.

Golden Pool

The fact that streams of opportunity flow past your front door is important, but being able to collect that energy renders the water course truly useful and so yokes "good" *feng shui* to the building. The qualities of openness, hollowness and constructive limitation are descriptive of effective golden pools. Structures or rooms that let an ample flow of *qi* in the front, collect some of that energy and allow the rest to flow on out the room and through the building and site, taking proper advantage of a water course.

The Spirit's Hearth

All residences have been built to house people, but the aspirations of each person are different. Therefore, you should judge the *feng shui* of your own place according to the extent that it furthers attainment of your life goals. Each place needs a physical space that symbolizes the aspirations of its occupant and that serves as a focal point from which to create those aspirations and ascend. Pagodas and mediaeval churches have spires that focus that energy. Japanese homes often have *tokunoma,* a focal alcove in which poignant calligraphy or *ikebana* is displayed to elevate the heart and mind. Some homes contain a shrine or altar place, while some devote an entire room to serve as a spiritual hearth.

Transformational Space

Within any building, there is continuous and dynamic change, except briefly in the apartments of the old who are near death. One building should not be able to hold a human being for an entire lifetime, because as you create personal transformation, *feng shui* changes simultaneously. If the degree of change in your fortunes or determination is substantial, no reasonable amount of altering your current home or office will alter the energy field enough to permit you to remain long. A building with "good" *feng shui* then will have the power to move you out its doors and into the next phase of life harmoniously. The closest physical characteristic of this quality is the feel of empty space. Sometimes transformational space is the garden, well known in both China and Japan for beauty and harmony. If you don't have a harmonious garden, you may sense transformational space in the pervasive but subtle sense of dynamism in the air.

Another way to think of favorable *feng shui* is to consider that the aim of any building or room is to integrate the powers of the natural landscape and the neighboring buildings. In some instances it means shielding the building's inhabitants from energies negative to daily living or detrimental to the accomplishment of cherished goals. In some instances it means yoking the positive opportunities latent in a place to the higher aspirations of those who live or work there. This process is very much like tuning a guitar or piano. The landscape is the instrument; the building and its rooms are the strings. The goals of the inhabitants are the precise pitch of the notes. Although a piano can be tuned, it takes a musician to play it. In this case, the building's tenants are the musicians who may have little or great skill at the art of living harmoniously.

A more scientific description of favorable *feng shui* is that a building is an open system whose parameters are managed to maximize its inhabitants' goals. The system of a house is completely dependent on the system of the landscape in which it is placed. They are relative to each other. Good *feng shui* is also relative. For instance, if an environment has a great abundance of positive *qi,* then a house does not in normal times need to be efficient at storing and conserving *qi* for the benefit of the family. By contrast, if an environment has a scarce flow of *qi,* then it is absolutely necessary that a home or business office be able to collect and conserve *qi* in order to sustain its occupants' lifestyles. A building has bad *feng shui* if it does not respond adequately in a given environment to accomplish the aims of its occupants.

Feng shui is an assessment of a living and interactive system. Adopting a sense of empirical play is the best way to discover how to fine-tune your place. After all, your home or office is just the game board for your personal evolution.

The following section lists specific instances of good *feng shui*, like positioning the stove and sink in a kitchen and angling walkways to the front door of a home or office. These are general rules that do not take into account that each and every part of a house-and-landscape system mutually effects the other. If you make a change someplace, such as putting furniture in a room so open it bleeds *qi,* it may have several effects, expected and unexpected.

Rules of Thumb and Room

Order

The following discussion is presented more in the style of a cookbook, intended to provide simple formulas to achieve a desired result. It is not intended as a menu planner. It aims at leading you to improve the *feng shui* of your home or workplace room by room, and is offered as an introductory guide and a practical initiation. Like any learning, unless you ground it in the philosophic approach, extend your intuition and understanding of *qi,* and integrate it into your experience, this presentation will have limited value. That means sometimes it will work and sometimes it won't, because a complete picture cannot be shown here. Remember, your deepening understanding and continued play with *feng shui* will make it work with greater and greater frequency until you attain abiding wisdom beyond wisdom.

Entranceway

1. The entrances to a house or office are gates into the lives of those inside. It shows everything about them. The entrance connects the *yang* world of unlimited universal activity with the *yin* world of the limited lives within.

2. The approach should be easy and obvious to any visitor coming by foot or car, with a clear, clean path indicated.

3. The entrance to any building should not face an oncoming lane, road, or thoroughfare.

4. The entrance should not be opposite a phone or power line pole, or face any corners or cutting structures, such as sharp edges and pointed shapes, nearby or in the distance.

5. If a house is walled, the walls should be proportionally distant from the front door. The gate in the wall should be obvious, as should the path to the front door from the gate.

6. The front yard should be maintained in good order. Trees and plants should be healthy. If a tree or a limb dies, remove it at once. Prune trees and bushes to prevent them from becoming entangled jumbles of limbs or from overpowering the building.

7. There should be a pedestrian path independent of a driveway from the property front to the main door. That path must be clean and clear of any debris.

8. The front door should be proportional to the house size. Doors let *qi* in and out; they should seem permeable but not porous.

9. There should be one front entryway — never two doors. A double front door is harmonious only in a large house and only if both doors are exactly the same in color, height, and materials.

10. The front door should be clean and well maintained. If any thing becomes wrong, such as burned out lights, a broken or weathered door or decaying post materials, fix it immediately.

11. The front door should be at grade or slightly elevated, not sunken or underground.

12. If a stairway leads up to a front door, it should not be too steep or too high. The stairway should be a uniform width or may be somewhat wider at the bottom than at the top, never the reverse.

13. There should be a level, proportionate platform at the top of stairs that lead to the front door.

14. A building should not have a front door that faces a temple, church, shrine or graveyard. The door should not face establishments of violence (prisons, police stations, etc.) or of entertainment that dissipate energy (gambling houses, pool halls, etc.) Pay heed to what the front door faces and lets in.

15. The front and back doors should not be in direct line with each other. The front door should be larger than the back door or any other door.

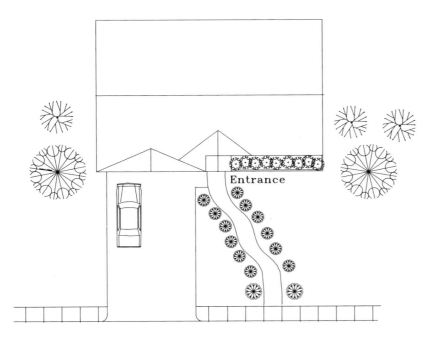

Entrance

The Entranceway

A meandering path directly from the sidewalk to the front entrance connects more energy to a house or office. The sidewalk is neccessary to connect the individual to the community.

16. The entrance hall or foyer should have but one door or arch leading to the next rooms and should be darker than the adjoining rooms.

17. Stairs to upper stories should not face the entrance foyer directly or even partly.

18. Upon entering a building, you should not be able to see a window to the back. Instead you should see a wall at a proportional distance.

19. Use works of art to set the tone for the whole house. Use subtle color and movement to welcome and direct your guests.

Living Room

20. The living room is analogous to the heart. It is a *yang* room, a public room, a gathering and show place. It should be adjacent to the entry.

21. The condition of the living room reflects the finances, status, and careers of its inhabitants. It draws or repels helpful guests, friends and relatives. It collects or disperses the energy of the whole family.

22. The feeling of the room should be one of activity and security. Walls of windows will only disperse *qi* and fortune. It should be separate from, not open to, other rooms.

23. Display your most beautiful, inspiring, or profound art in the living room. Avoid displaying antiques from temples or armories as they may have residual, inharmonious *qi*.

24. The living room should be on the same level as the entry, not sunken.

25. The living room should be well lighted, not necessarily from too many windows. It should have bright light even at night.

26. Upon entering the house, the fireplace should not be visible. Fireplaces radiate *qi,* but when not it use they also disperse it. Have tight fireplace doors that eliminate chimney updrafts and *qi* leaks.

27. The household wealth corner is in the living room at a diagonal from the front door. The corner should not have a door or windows diminishing it. It is the main energy collection spot for the whole family.

28. Place something stable and alive in the wealth corner, never a mirror. If you place plants or fish there, do not move them about frequently.

29. Plants should be large enough to sit on the floor. None should hang from the ceiling or the walls.

30. Arrange the furniture so host and hostess sit with their backs to a wall. Guests may sit with their backs to doorways or windows.

31. Living room furniture should be arranged simply and elegantly, and be similar or complimentary in style, i.e. color, shape, size, period, etc.

32. Furniture should be arranged from low to high toward the focal point. Avoid making distracting juxtapositions of uneven pieces or causing irregular lines up and down.

33. If there are two sitting areas within the living room, one should be larger. The larger area should include the wealth corner.

The Wealth Corner

When entering a living room, you will find the wealth corner located diagonally across the room from the door. It is best backed by solid walls to hold the resources of value to the household.

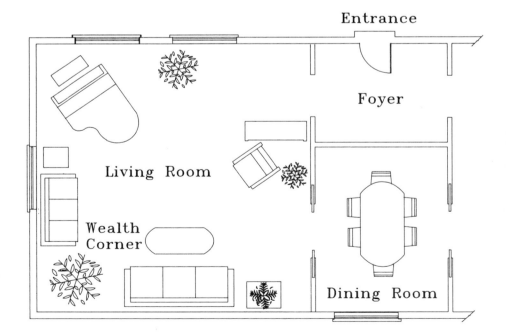

Kitchen

34. The kitchen is a *yang* room. It is analogous to the liver. It is the place of nurturing and support. At times it is public and at others it is private.

35. In the kitchen, the two agents of water and fire are used to blend the five tastes of the five agents *(wu xing)*. It is imperative that fire (stove, oven and microwave) and water (sink) be balanced.

36. Sink and stove may be next to one another or on the same wall, at a 90° or 120° angle apart, but never directly opposite one another.

37. The sink may be below a window but the stove should never be.

38. The stove should not be visible from the front door and should not have a door either to the right or left of it or directly behind.

39. After orientation to the doorways, a stove is placed more harmoniously facing east or south, the directions of the sun.

40. If the stove is set in an island in the middle of the kitchen, it will always be in opposition to the sink. Husband and wife will fight.

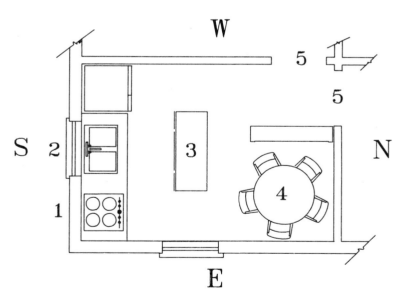

The Kitchen

41. The most favorable arrangement is for the stove to be supported by two walls, located at or near a corner.

42. The kitchen should not have sky lights, especially not above the stove. The kitchen should not have a high ceiling.

43. The kitchen shape should be a regular square or rectangle. Avoid semicircular and L-shaped arrangements.

1. The stove is in the wealth corner and is protected from traffic. 2. The sink can be on the same wall as the stove and can be under a window. 3. A counter provides a place to prepare food and protects the cook's security. 4. The round table spins traffic away from the inner kitchen. Two solid walls protect those eating at the kitchen table. 5. Norin, $^1/_3$-height doorway curtains, slow traffic through the kitchen and protect the cook and those eating at the table.

Dining Room

44. The dining room is analogous to the spleen and is a *yang* room. Nothing in its decor should divert attention from food and nurturing conversation.

45. While eating, many different "foods" are eaten, including inspiration to the spirit. Therefore, color and artwork should invoke the harmonious aspirations of family members. Nothing there should startle. The room should be free of messes and kept clean.

46. The dining room is less *yang* than the kitchen or living room and needs balance from *yin* in order to be a more comfortable place in which to linger.

47. The dining room should have an intimate feel. Avoid having three doors and a window in the four walls.

48. The chairs of family members should always back against a wall. Most of the chairs should have a windowless wall as backup.

49. Practical kitchen utensils should not be stored or left in the dining room in open view.

Study, Studio or Office

50. In a home or a business, a study or office is a *yang* room, but requires balance from *yin* to focus the energy for an extended period of time. The correct balance depends on the room's purpose. If there are many meetings there, more *yang* is required; if more study or reading is done there, more *yin* is needed for individual focus.

51. In a home, if the study is a place to receive business visitors, it should be close to the front door.

52. A desk should be backed up by a solid wall or piece of furniture showing stability. It should not be against a window, a mirror, or a corner.

53. The desk should not be in direct line facing the doorway, or have the door to the immediate right or left.

54. The desk should not be placed at 30° to 60° angles to the walls, rather the desk should be parallel and square to the walls.

55. The room shape should be square or rectangular. In a creative office, furniture with curves and ovals is better. In a money management office, square furniture is better.

56. There should not be a pathway behind a desk, or a door opening from the rear, or a window behind the desk.

57. Neither plants nor lights should be hung above a desk.

58. The diagonal corner from the door to an office is its wealth corner. The same rules for a wealth corner in the living room are applicable here. If possible, place the desk in the wealth corner.

59. In a commercial building, the offices of the CEO and CFO should be located on the left side of the building as you look out.

60. The front door of a commercial building should have a door larger than the front door of a residence. Within a building, an office complex should have a door larger than a residence, but in proportion to its size.

61. A commercial building should be a square or a proportional rectangle, not too narrow.

62. In the five agents *(wu xing),* the square corresponds to the color yellow and earth, which gives direct rise to metal (gold or money). Earth is the ally of all commerce. Water is the medium of trade.

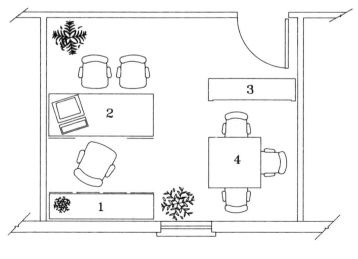

The Office

63. Avoid triangular buildings for any part of a normal business or manufacturing concern. A triangle corresponds to red and among the *wu xing* to fire. Fire destroys metal and is an enemy of income.

64. The office of the CEO is the microcosm of the entire company. It should be square or rectangular, hold energy yet circulate energy to the various departments. The ceiling should be elevated over the CEO's desk. The room's focus should be the CEO's desk.

1. The credenza facing out should be low. It sits in the wealth corner of this office. 2. You should sit facing the door's direction but not directly in its path. Your back should be against solid, unadorned walls. 3. Bookshelves stop the uncomfortable *qi* to create a secure area beyond. 4. This manager deals in detail work. The square table helps handle plodding progress with care.

65. The wall behind a desk should be plain so a visitor focuses on the person at the desk and does not become distracted by a stunning view or unusual artwork. This is doubly true of a CEO's office.

66. To put a visitor's chair with its back to a door or window is to put him or her in a disadvantageous and defensive position.

67. When entering an office, you should face a wall, never a window. The wall may have a floor plant or art work to draw visitors and *qi* inside it.

Bedrooms

68. All bedrooms are *yin* rooms. They are analogous to the lungs. They are places of rest and peace. They are places where the mind wanders from the body in search of astral experience.

69. The bedroom should be more square than rectangular, and the shapes of furniture therein should be either. Avoid circles.

70. The bed should not be in a direct line with or at a right angle to the door. The path of energy should not intersect the bed. The line of *qi* should flow in from the door without obstruction from the bed.

71. The head of the bed should be backed up by a wall, never a window or a mirrored wall.

72. Light should come from either right or left, but the sides of the head of the bed should not be directly exposed to a window.

73. Nothing should be above the bed on the ceiling, such as a skylight, a beam, a hanging lamp or plant.

74. Limit mirrors in the bedroom to one or none. Do not place a mirror so it is directly at the foot of the bed.

75. Orient the head of the bed to the north or facing east only when such placement is not in the paths of doors or windows (used or not used) that would disturb the sleepers' *qi.*

76. Do not place a bed under a slanting, low ceiling. It will oppress.

77. Bedroom ceilings should not be high lest the sleeper's *qi* be dispersed into too much space. A mirror above the bed likewise will diffuse *qi.*

78. Low ceilings and compact walls should be painted light colors to make them seem to recede. High ceilings and distant walls should be painted darker colors to make them appear closer.

79. The master bedroom should be determined not by size, but by the quality of *qi* there. Little *qi* in a master bedroom leads to fewer children and an unhappy marriage.

80. Master bedrooms should not contain vast spaces or have entertainment centers, fireplaces, wet bars, etc.

81. A bedroom should feel secure and intimate, but not confining.

82. Bedrooms should not have a TV as it disturbs the sleeper's *qi*. If a TV happens to be in a hotel room, never go to sleep with it on. Before retiring, cover it with very opaque material if it can't be shut in a wood cabinet with doors.

83. Decorate bedrooms in subdued, subtle tones with inspiring artwork. Avoid many electronic devices and electric colors.

84. The placement of the bed should be above the floor at least one hand's length. It should not be higher than two feet.

85. When facing the bed, you should not be able to look under it. If you can, cover it so that it appears solid.

86. Bedrooms should be at the back of the house, removed from the activity of daily living. They are a retreat.

87. Do not use beds with round posts, canopies, or bulbous decorations.

88. If a bed is an antique, it may have residual negative *qi*. If it does, do not sleep in it.

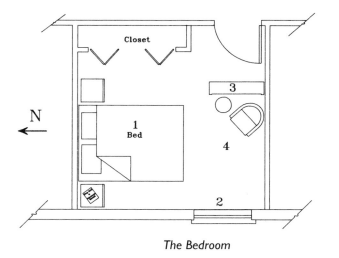

The Bedroom

1. The couple lie feet facing the door, protected in the wealth corner. Their heads at the north improve dream insight. 2. Few windows are needed in a sleep-and-dream room. No windows should cross the bed. 3. Bookshelves or high dressers (six feet) block the doorway energy and contribute to repose. 4. The protected area is perfect for a reading, conversation or meditation area. It is also good for a personal or family shrine.

89. When moving to a new home, obtain a new bed and bedding. Failing that, obtain a new mattress. Failing that, at least purchase new sheets and pillows.

90. Near the head of the bed, keep written aspirations and inspirational sayings and pictures. Contemplate them at least briefly before going to sleep and again upon waking.

Shrine Rooms

91. If your house is large enough, you ought to have a shrine room in which to do meditation, visualization and spiritual practices consistent with your beliefs.

92. A shrine room is a *yin* room, a place to nourish your highest aspirations. It is the focal point for your life goals. It is the place from which you will ascend.

93. A family shrine, altar or *butsudan* should not be located in the direct path of a door or in front of a window. A high transom window is acceptable above the altar.

94. The altar should be solid, decorated with a cloth, surrounded perhaps by symbols of the *wu xing* and your personal symbols for aspiration. It may contain art depicting your highest visualization of the embodied divine.

95. The shrine room may be incorporated into a bedroom, but should occupy a solid corner, such as the wealth corner.

Bathrooms

96. Bathrooms and toilet rooms are *yin* rooms. They are analogous to the kidneys. They are places of personal purification.

97. All sinks, faucets and toilets should be in good working order. If they leak, fix them immediately. It is a sign of leaking finances.

98. All bathroom fixtures should be clean. The room should be pleasant and simple.

99. Never locate a shower or bath tub by a large window, either opaque or clear. The room should have light, but not too much. It should feel secure, but not spacious.

Hallways

100. Long, straight halls accelerate *qi* to a negative rate. In long, wide halls, use hanging curtains, darker colors, or matte finishes or furniture placement to slow *qi*. In short or confining halls, use light colors and reflective surfaces and remove furniture to open up the energy.

101. When several doorways open to the same hallway, they should never directly or partially face one another. A door out of a room should open onto a wall that is blank or directly to an art work.

102. Hallways should feel neither confining nor too vacant. Halls are the meridians between *yin* and *yang* rooms. They regulate the pace of the house or building and should reflect balance.

103. Hallways should not pass through the middle of other rooms.

Decorations and Symbols

104. Plants and aquariums purify inharmonious energies, while drawing and collecting life energy to them and to the room they occupy. Tend them well so they are healthy. If a plant or fish dies, replace it immediately.

105. Mirrors are symbols of the unobstructed, empty nature of mind. They open up *qi* in confined space. They also can reflect too much light in a bright or vast space. Too many mirrors in one place can further confuse the distinction between real and illusory. Mirrors reflect back inharmonious energies pointed at your home or business.

106. Any art work displayed in your home or office should evoke positivity, awe, creativity, peace or inspiration. Art and decorations should mean something intense to you. Decor should not be used merely to avoid emptiness or simplicity. Both works of art and artful emptiness display the state and depth of your spirit.

107. The *feng shui* of your place is symbolic of your life, revealing alike to self and guests. It addresses different levels of the mind at the same time. It is in constant change. It shadows the unseen: the future.

108. Ponder the rationale for each of these rules of thumb. You can perceive and understand the mandala of anyone's place. You can transform your place into a wish-fulfilling gem. *Aum mani padme hung!*

Feng Shui Diagnosis

Look

The following areas need to be investigated as you assess the overall harmony or disharmony of a space — whether an empty site, office, shop, home, corporate headquarters, hotel, or industrial building. Each area needs to be integrated so you can establish and communicate a plan that matches the resources available to bring change. The following steps are presented as if you are diagnosing someone else's space, because it helps you to be objective if you think of the space as belonging to someone else. Methodically apply each step, so you won't miss something of great importance.

1. Take a history. Find out what has happened in that place, in that section of the city or town, in that building, in each of its rooms, to each of the members of a family or members of the management team, or to the key inhabitants. Ask about the history of the property in as much detail as possible. Learn what is done in each room. Sometimes the room triggers deep, insightful or emotional memories that reveal much. Most importantly, ask the inhabitants what their goals in life are, long and short term. Later you can correlate this information to confirm or deny your other impressions.

2. Examine form and line. Examine the surrounding terrain for landforms. Assess the building shape. It helps to draw a map with measurements or to contemplate a proportional floor plan. Note the shapes of the rooms, relations of doors, windows, arches, apertures and hallways.

3. Feel *qi*, its strength and flow. Make a direct assessment of the sensations, feelings, thought forms, auras, presences and character of the energy field room by room and overall.

4. Check directions. Note the direction each room faces. After dividing the building and its lot into nine squares, correlate room uses with the eight directions, using the River Lo Map. If there is more than one story, apply the diagram to each level.

5. See and contemplate the meaning of symbols present. Examine the knick-knacks, pictures, art works, furniture styles, fabrics, colors, and appointments of each room, public and private. Include the building and site exterior in your survey. Does the symbology confirm or deny your other evaluations?

6. Examine water. Check the plumbing, sinks, bathtubs, showers, drinking water quality, pools, spas, fountains. Ask about any history of leaks if you can't discover any by inspection. Next examine the flow of activity by gravity, slope positions, business-related movement, street life, profusion or dearth of vegetation. Make a judgment about the amount of nurturing resources flowing to the building and the amount retained.

7. Examine wind. Inquire about weather patterns, especially wind. Find out if there are any unique patterns to the building or to the local area. Check the site and building for erosion. Also check power lines and microwave radiation emitted in the building or nearby. Inquire as to the nearest garbage, toxic, chemical, radiation or waste water dump sites. If near such a site, consult a topographical map or other descriptive material so you can assess the danger. In the house, note the placement of electrical outlets in problem rooms.

8. Consult other systems on difficult questions. Sometimes you will not be able to form a coherent opinion of the nature of particular causes or effects. *Feng shui* cures cannot dissolve pre-existing lifelong karma, though it may be able to soften the impact of difficult life patterns. An outside system, like divination using the *I Ching* or consulting astrology, will often clarify whether the condition you are aiming to cure is conditioned by life karma, time or place. You can thereafter determine whether it can be dissolved and how to go about it. Astrology, Chinese, Western and Hindu, can offer insight into all these questions. There are even branches of Western astrology dealing with the effects of place. One is called "Astro*Carto*Graphy"®, another is called "local space." Conclusions based on these systems can offer confirmation of an analysis, show a blind spot in your assessment, or reveal an intractable limitation. When two systems agree, act; when three agree, hurry!

9. What is your overall impression? Take time to sort out your assessments and integrate them into an understandable statement. Do not ignore how the building and its occupants relate to life around their place (human, animal, vegetable, mineral, and astral). Rank the building's problems by the priority of their seriousness. You must tune the building to the goals of its inhabitants no matter whether you think they are foolish or wise in their choices. Gently, you may encourage them toward higher aspiration. If they make any change with positive, conscious intent, they are moving in the right direction.

10. Limit cures to seven. The last phase is more creative problem solving than analysis and requires the free play of your imagination, experience and assessment of the site. Talk about the seven most important things that need change in order to bring the building into greater harmony with the occupants' aspirations. If they say it can't be done, suggest at least two other (and perhaps cheaper ways) that the problem can be resolved or at least ameliorated somewhat. Inspire the will to change positively and support the method of that change using the depths of your skill, wisdom and compassion. Engage their special creativity in counterbalancing or augmenting *feng shui* weaknesses or strengths.

What's Wrong With America's Homes and Offices?

Home

Every office, home and plot or parcel of land is unique. It is therefore a dangerous generalization to categorize all American buildings and their sites as exhibiting the same characteristics that reveal the modern character of Americans. Nevertheless, certain themes are repeated, especially in buildings that have been built during the past generation. Below is a quick list of what to watch for as you evaluate your own spaces for harmony with heaven and earth.

1. The garage is the grand approach. It ought to be clear where human beings should enter a home or office building. Often the only clear path is the double driveway to the garage, with a walkway to the front door either forgotten or an afterthought. Cars and transportation are of pre-eminent value to persons living or working in places of this type. Life is lived in a freeway lane, fast or slow.

2. The gate that hides the spirit. Houses and offices that have their front doors hidden reveal one of several things about the occupants: (a) they want to hide from friends, family and community, (b) they do not have a basic focal point or are trying to hide their life's focal point; or, (c) they are not receiving the nourishment they need in the critical phases of their lives.

3. Disjunctive shapes attract shapeless lives. Architects give home buyers what they want: unique spaces that became even more unusual by incorporating irregular shapes and angles into the floor plan. The usual house or office shape is now a highly irregular 3-D polyhedron. The people inside mirror the shape and have highly disjunctive lifestyles that tear them apart with stress. The areas of life most out of tune are reflected in the rooms most out of shape.

4. Let them eat *qi*. There are two popular kitchen types, one that is more like a hallway, a route to somewhere else, and one that is arrayed in the open concept. The hallway kitchen means family nurturing is hampered because the cook is always assaulted in the kitchen. If the cook doesn't want to cook, meals slack off in taste, nutrition, creativity and *prana*. The open concept, although different in arrangement, means the cook is constantly distracted by other household matters. Food preparation also suffers, since it is dispersed into the great open space. In both cases, not only food but other forms of nurturing are lacking — money, affection, "quality time," learning and skill.

5. Let them eat . . . somewhere else. Dining rooms these days are usually at a crossroads. If there are four walls, at least three of them have openings, and sometimes there are four openings: a door from the kitchen, a double door from the living room, a sliding glass door to the deck or pool, and a window to show the views. Consequently, each position is uncomfortable for formal dining. As a result, if there are dinner parties, they quickly adjourn to another place after jittery conversation. The family does not focus itself on the daily ritual of mutual nurturing. Most likely the room isn't used at all, except as a collection place for papers, clothing, and mess.

6. My master bedroom is my castle. Master bedrooms are quickly eclipsing kitchen-dining-family rooms as being the largest space complex in a house measured in square feet. So much activity in terms of TV's, stereos, fireplaces, conversation pits, window walls with vistas, closet rooms, washing complexes, and toilet rooms are so juxtaposed and joined that not much rest or intimacy can take place in these vast areas. It is ironic to consider the effects these "entertainment" master rooms have: divorce rates have become directly proportional to the square footage consumed by master bedrooms. It must not be the right approach to lasting relationships because it isn't working.

7. People who live in glass houses shouldn't. A recent trend in architecture seems to be to fill external walls with as many square feet of glass as possible. This is true of offices and homes. Windows and glass let light in and let *qi* out. Corners are places where *qi* accumulates, but if the corner is at a junction of two windows, *qi,* resources and money leak out of the house. Why is America a debtor nation? Too many windows in all the wrong places at home and work.

8. Long lines over open space accelerate life's pace! The longer a straight line, whether a hallway, walkway, or defined line across open space, the greater the acceleration of *qi* and consequently the greater the pace of your life. Any uninterrupted stretch of straight lines outside (telephone wires, radio towers, or lines of adjacent buildings) will aim accelerated energy called *sha qi* into your home or office. That *qi* will either disrupt or further accelerate your life's pace. American homes and offices suffer both by design (architectural) and by neighboring chance from this BIG problem.

9. "You're not investing in a home, you're buying a lifestyle." In general, American homes are not designed to foster family cohesion or to create a sense of community within or without, and neither are business buildings. Instead, they tend to isolate the individual and break down the social fabric that existed just one generation ago. There are no longer "homemakers" because it is considered socially inferior to devote oneself to tending the hearth of Vesta. The truth is there are no places where homemakers can nurture or be nurtured. So, all of us go off to the malls, the arenas, and the courts (divorce and tennis).

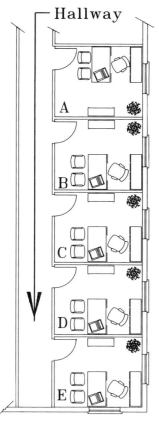

Hallway

Hallways

A hallway that is too long speeds up *qi*. In this configuration, whoever occupies rooms C and D will not get much attention. Room A gets too much; room B is in the favored position. Room E at the end of the line may be oversupervised. That room could be occupied by the eldest child in a house, or an employee who doesn't fit in and is on the way out.

Feng Shui Cures for the Common Home

Aim

What can be done to fix "bad" or inharmonious *feng shui?* There are a number of cures that can be administered with differing degrees of success. There are three aspects to applying cures to the *qi* field energy that a house or office building radiates. The first is that the moment a change is created, it is at that moment the *qi* field changes. Although Western science had assumed until quite recently that experiments are 100% repeatable, Chinese science knows better. Once something is done, no matter how small, it changes everything, even if it seems imperceptible. This means any cure applied to a building will change it, but will it be acceptable and will it be enough?

The second aspect of creating *feng shui* cures is that the measure of success lies in between the perceptions and limitations of the inhabitants. For example, a person may expect that if she moves a couch from a window, she will win a large lottery prize. On the other hand, the same person may be incapable of making a prescribed change, like blocking a window diagnosed as causing money leaks. If, after two months, there is a $250 monthly increase in household money from the limited cures applied, the same person may regard this as too trivial to notice or report. In short, it requires a lot of investigation to gauge how effective cures actually are.

The third aspect of *feng shui* cures is to learn to play with them. Often there are several cures that will improve a situation: one that is too costly in time or money, one that feels funny, and one that elicits some enthusiasm. There are more and less effective cures just as some cures will be more or less threatening. Engage in a problem-solving dialogue with those living or working in that space. The purpose of problem-solving play is to show them what is wrong, to persuade and motivate them to do something, and to engage their own creativity to loosen the limitations the place imposes upon them.

How long will it take a cure to take effect? After making intended changes, within three to seven days there will be signs, subtle intimations and omens as to the cures' effectiveness. Within one month (the next new moon to full moon), events will develop and opportunities appear that are new. After three months, the full promises of the changes will show themselves. If after one season you feel the change not far-reaching enough, then it is time to reevaluate the *feng shui* and institute other changes, perhaps even changes that last time seemed too expensive, funny, or radical. The effect of the cure, however, is dependent on three factors: intent, intensity, and duration. Intent is discussed in the following section. You must apply a cure force equal to the force of the problem, combining greater intensity or longer duration to counterbalance.

1. Awareness is all. Like any other field requiring diagnosis, such as acupuncture, car repair or debugging software, the course of action to be taken depends on the thoroughness of the diagnosis. In *feng shui* it also depends on the awareness of the person inhabiting a place. If a *feng shui* expert can see something about another's business or personal life, but fails to make him aware of it, the cures applied may be less effective for harmonious change. Conversely, if a *feng shui* practitioner of lesser skill suggests a crude cure, but if the woman making the change is very aware, the cure will be more effective than an expert would expect. The intent of the inhabitant and how well it is focused has a great deal to do with the cure's effect and seems to heighten or lessen the intensity of the cure applied.

2. Move out and up! The most dramatic cure is to move out of your present business or home and into a new life in a place with better *feng shui.* Three conditions especially warrant this approach: (1) The current place is so limiting that cures will produce little relief or joy while costing too much in money, time, and trouble; (2) you need an entirely new perspective because you have become so comfortable or so confused as to lose the sense of creativity and joy in life; (3) major change is occurring in the neighborhood so that *feng shui* of your place is unduly injured, but over which you have no control.

3. Revise and remodel? Before you set out to remodel a place to improve its *feng shui,* make certain the change will be beneficial. It is possible through the addition of an extraneous angle, room or wing to injure the *feng shui* of a building. Remodeling is a tricky prospect because architects, engineers, contractors, carpenters, electricians and plumbers will try to influence your intent so that it is easier for them to do, or so they can execute it using current technology. Also be aware that for a period of three months to one year, depending on how much of the building and grounds were changed, there will be unsettled *qi* and therefore the affairs of those inside will be unsettled temporarily before you can realistically review the effects of the change clearly. If a building lacks the proper focus or approach or if a major deficiency exists, there is no choice but to remodel (or move).

When someone menaces you with a pointed finger, that is *sha qi* deliberately thrown your way. Any time energy (*qi,* electric, kinetic, thermal) accelerates along a line, the result is *sha qi.* Linear *sha qi* is so strong, pointed and quick that it injures life, which is circular energy.

4. To escape, or to landscape? Many *feng shui* problems start in the front yard before you can ever find the front door. The main landscape change is to open up access to the front door for pedestrians, unless your entire life is drive-through. Next most common is to use trees, bushes and shrubs to break up *sha qi,* which are injurious energies directed at your property by roads, neighboring buildings, TV towers or electrical power lines. Think of your yard as an experiment in bringing you what you want in life, so choose flowers, foliage, and colors with an eye to expressing your innermost and highest aspiration where you and everyone else can see them.

5. Redecorate and rearrange. Seemingly, the least expensive way to create *feng shui* change is to rearrange what you already have. As soon as you start, though, you will realize that what you already own is dead (as far as symbolic motivation for you is concerned), or that you don't have the right furniture, art works, or decorative themes. Screens, bookcases and *norin* (doorway drapes) are handy to block and redirect *qi*. Art work, plants and inviting furniture are good to draw *qi* and people to certain spots you want them to approach. Start rearranging slowly, and get one piece of furniture, or art work at a time. Rarely will you get it right the first time, so adopt a sense of play and fiscal conservatism in acquiring the new. Then sell or donate the old things you replaced because there is no room for them in your remodeled life.

6. Ritual. The great subconscious mind communicates in symbols and so do rituals. Through performing rituals, which need not be elaborate but should be focused, you will change things at a mind level upstream to the physical house or office in which you live. Rituals can free energy to make other changes, or to allow you to view things with less indecision and with greater clarity and compassion. The most primal ritual is purification, which may consist of you cleaning your house every Monday, or doing spring cleaning right before the vernal equinox. A life-focus ritual is described in a subsequent section. There are other rituals you can do, but all of them will contribute to the sense that your home or office is a sacred place in which you, the vast, light-filled, compassionate one, temporarily dwell.

7. Mandala. Attuning your home or office to the divine so that it imitates the plan of creation is the most sweeping change to make because it causes a person, family or company to redo the internal and external worlds at the same time. It also cannot be accomplished in one quick sweep through the premises. Evaluation and change must be continuous and steady. On the following page, you will find the River Lo Map that correlates the eight directions, the trigrams of the *I Ching,* time, season, color, number and activity. This map or mandala is linked to the great *gua*, the Well, presented earlier. By contemplating this arrangement, you can make changes in your home, office or land that correspond to the River Lo arrangement. You can also use this tool for diagnosis, but remember that the flow of *qi* is the primary and the River Lo mandala is a secondary symbolic representation. Physical things like furniture, walls and land are tertiary.

The River Lo Map and the Eight Directions

4	9	2
Southeast Morning Midspring	South Noon Summer	Southwest Afternoon Midsummer
Xun: The Gentle Wind or Wood Red and Green Wealth, Resources	*Li:* The Clinging Fire Red Fame, Status, Tradition	*Kun:* The Receptive Earth Red and White, Pink Marriage, Relationship
East Dawn Spring	Center Timeless Eternal moment	West Dusk Autumn
3	**5**	**7**
Zhen: The Arousing Thunder Green or Blue-green Family, Clan, Community	*Tao:* The Way Middle Yellow Origin, Return, End	*Dui:* The Joyous Lake White Children, Pleasures
Northeast Predawn Night Midwinter	North Midnight Winter	Northwest Evening Midautumn
Gen: Keeping Still Mountain Green and Black Knowledge, Skill	*Kan:* The Abysmal Water Indigo or Black Career, Destiny, Innovation	*Qian:* The Creative Heaven, Sky, Deep Space White and Black, Gray Helpful People, Friends
8	**1**	**6**

Life Focus Ritual

One heart, one mind

A symptom in many offices, homes or stores is that so many objects are displayed that the beauty of any one of them is drowned in the sea of too many. The simplest *feng shui* ritual is to purge your home regularly of items you don't really use or that no longer mean anything to you. The best time is at proverbial spring cleaning time, near the vernal equinox. The next best time is at your birthday. Next best is at any new moon. Next best after that is right now. Usually you can start with the things you like least in order to make some easy progress in ridding yourself of unwanted baggage. Unfortunately, proceeding backwards isn't an effective method for removing all the scattering influences, memories, illusions and diversions from your life.

For any process of *feng shui* to be effective, you have to know to what vibration you are attuning a house, garden or office. What is the middle C of the life you want to live? To find that vibration means to clear everything else away so you can make the decision of what you want most. You won't have to agonize over the choice of an east or a south facing door if in advance you know what you are seeking. The most direct path is to choose what you want most to accomplish, and then make everything else resonate to it. Tune every form, direction, symbol and energy complex in your house and office toward attaining your goal. You will easily attain that goal in a short time.

The reason for choosing one goal is simple mathematics of the alternative. It takes a certain amount of energy to activate a dream in the real world. The amount of energy needed is a product of the amount of time you nurture a goal and the intensity with which you go about that nurturing. If it takes three hours a day for three months of intense concentration to make something manifest for you, consider how long it will take if you are shifting your attention among forty-nine things. The time to incubate all those goals would be at least twelve years and three months, assuming you don't add new things during that time. It also assumes you won't throw away one of the forty-nine aspirations before they bloom. Rather than cultivate infinite patience in the face of frustration, it is much simpler to take three months to choose and nourish one goal. Then you can see if it works and you waste no time in adjusting the *feng shui* back and forth among a menu of goals.

The next page lists easy steps for you to follow in order to combine your reason, intuition and imagination together to concentrate your conscious and unconscious energies toward attaining what you want. Of course, choosing the wisest goal for you is part of this art. The most subtle skill of the Way of Wind and Water is in learning to make one wise choice after another.

Ritual Steps

1. Contemplate your life. Write down the seven most important goals you want to accomplish in your lifetime.

2. Contemplate your life. Cross off four goals.

3. Contemplate your life. Choose one of the three remaining goals that you will focus your energy toward completing in the next six months.

4. Make an altar in an intimate, comfortable place in your home. Place symbols on the altar of the goal you are trying to realize. Place a picture of your highest image of an embodied divine being at the center. You may also light candles and incense and place symbols of the five agents there.

5. Write your goal on several pieces of paper. Place one on your altar, one in your wallet or purse, one in your car, one on your desk and one at your bedside. Repeat this goal as an affirmation as many times a day as possible, but minimally upon waking and just before going to sleep. Begin this ritual on the new moon, or at the vernal or autumnal equinox and continue for three months. Intensify your practice on new and full moon days.

6. At least once a day, at rising or before retiring, visualize an image of your deity three feet in front of you and slightly above your eyebrows. Visualize your deity radiating light rays into your head, throat and heart that confer upon you the power to accomplish your goal harmoniously. Absorb so many light rays from the inexhaustible source that you begin to radiate back rays of wisdom, compassion and accomplishment of your goal in all directions without limit. Then, let the deity dissolve indistinguishably into your being. Sit quietly for a few moments.

7. Throughout the day when you recite your goal, recall the feeling of radiating the power of positive accomplishment of your goal.

8. At the end of three lunar months, your life will have changed positively in the direction you have chosen. You may notice (1) a change in the outside world precipitating some event; (2) an unmistakable surge of qi in your spinal column; (3) satisfaction with your progress toward accomplishing your goal; or (4) no more motivation to continue this ritual.

9. Re-evaluate your life progress in the last three months. Start this process again at number one above. In the last three months your life goals may have changed. What has come to you and what has fallen easily away?

Feng Shui Tao: Learning Skills and Knowledge for Mastery

As in almost any learning field, from professional practice to games, you can learn in many different ways. Lessons are spiritual, intellectual, emotional and practical. Those who master a subject integrate learning experiences from all four of these areas into a coherent view, yet continue to remain open to more learning. Educational psychology reveals that there is no one best way to learn because people process information and experience differently. Educational psychology further reveals that whatever the subject matter, what you need most in order to learn is desire for knowledge coupled with perseverance. This is remarkably like advice from the Judgment text of the *I Ching* from the *gua,* the Well.

There is no one best way to learn the art of *Feng Shui Tao.* Also, there is no one manner in which to practice *Feng Shui Tao.* There is an almost infinite variety of possibilities. Given the information presented here and what you may already know, you should have a basic understanding of *feng shui.* It is always best to learn from a good teacher in order to continue your education. With or without a teacher physically present, an important part of your learning process will be to integrate experiences you have had in the past into the framework of *feng shui.* Remember that, as with any new study, you will need to explore and test this new field, too.

On the next page is a table that shows areas of learning, both Eastern and Western, that I believe are relevant to *feng shui.* You don't need mastery or even familiarity with most of them. If you find an area in which you have some, or even considerable experience, try to relate what you know already to what you have just learned. One thing you may discover is that you have a considerable store of knowledge which you are now about to view from a different perspective. That act alone may open a great reservoir of discovery as well as confidence that you can understand this field.

Learning

A second use of the table is to suggest areas of study. I recommend choosing subjects from the Eastern side of the ledger if you want to learn *feng shui.* Pick a subject in which you already have an interest so your own native enthusiasm will make learning more like play. Secondly, pick a subject for which there are some resources available locally, especially teachers of that tradition. As you pursue the angle of your interest, even if it is just reading a magazine article for general familiarity, other related areas of inquiry will open up. Also, the section after this contains a list of books that may be helpful. Learn with a sense of play, openness and wonder and you will learn *feng shui* well enough to improve your life personally and professionally.

Ways, Skills and Knowledge	Eastern	Western
Self-Cultivation Methods	*Qi Gong;* Meditation: *zazen, koan,* diety, *mantrayana, hua tou, mahamudra, dzogchen;* Yoga: *yantra, hatha, kriya, karma, jnana, tantra, raja, pranayama, puja,* etc.	Prayer, ritual, ESP, Contemplation, asceticism
Philosophy	*Yin/Yang,* Taoist, Confucian, Buddhist, Vedic	Greek, Egyptian, comparative, occult, scientific
Literature	*I CHING, LI CHING, (Ta Hsueh and Chung Yung) SHU CHING, SHIH CHING, YUEH CHING,* SPRING AND AUTUMN ANNALS, *KUNG FU TZU* ANALECTS, *TAO TE CHING, CHAUNG TZU*	Poetry, comparative literature, Shakespeare
Sacred and Fine Arts	Painting, poetry *(Kado),* music, *(Shakuhachi, ching, etc.)* tea ceremony *(Chado),* calligraphy, *Ikebana, bonsai,* gardening, sculpture, *thangkas, mandalas,* sacred dance, *Kabuki* and *Noh* theatre	Painting, drawing, music, sculpture, dance, poetry, theater
Language	Chinese, Japanese, Korean, Tibetan, Thai, Sanskrit, Classic Chinese, Mongolian, Manchu	Sumerian, Egyptian, Hebrew, Greek, Latin, Basque, Celtic, Old English, Old French, Persian
Healing	*Jing-lo* system, herbs, acupuncture, *tui na, shiatsu, kiatsu,* diet, anatomy of astral bodies and *nadis, ayurveda*	Anatomy, physiology, massage and touch therapies, nutrition, genetics, psychology, counseling, herbology
Martial Arts	*Bushido, Tai-chi, Kung-fu, Hsing-i, Ba-gua, Aikido, Iaido, Kyudo, Kendo, Judo,* ART OF WAR *(Strategy)*	Military strategy, strategic planning, marketing, organizational behavior
Craft Ways *(Tao or Do)*	Carpentry/architecture, pottery, paper making, sculpture, bell casting, *origami, shoji* (screen) making	Architecture, interior design, landscape design, gardening, farming, woodworking, building trades, graphic arts, pottery, glass blowing, leather working, goldsmithing, fountain design

Ways, Skills and Knowledge	Eastern	Western
Sciences	SCIENCE and CIVILIZATION IN ANCIENT CHINA, Needleman	Aerospace, astrophysics, biology, computer studies, ecology, engineering, gemology, geography, geohydrology, geology, meteorology, oceanography
Intuitive Arts	Astrology, almanacs, *Wu Xing*, divinations, system of forms, physiognomy, *Qi*-ESP, Taoist magic and alchemy	Astrology, numerology, tarot, dowsing, palm or face reading, geomancy, magic, alchemy
Domestic Arts	Cooking, "Art of Love," fabrics, dyeing, sewing, *norin*	Cooking, sewing, fashion design
Governance	History, Way of Heaven, social economy	History, law, urban planning, futurist studies, criminology, finance
Play	*Go, Shogi*	Hiking, mountaineering, sailing, football, tennis, basketball, baseball
Natural Resources		Industries of: mining, forestry, oil, water, pollution control, animal husbandry, civil engineering
Trade		Building contractors, realtors, land developers, furniture manufacturing and sales

Resources for Learning *Feng Shui*

Works Relating to *Feng Shui* and Geomancy

Literature

Eitel, Ernst (John Mitchell, commentary). **FENG-SHUI.**
Graham Brash Ltd., Singapore, 1984.

Grove, Durham. FENG SHUI AND WESTERN BUILDING CEREMONIES.
Graham Brash, Singapore, 1992.

Lip, Evelyn. FENG SHUI FOR BUSINESS.
Heian International, Union City, CA, 1990.

Lip, Evelyn. FENG SHUI FOR THE HOME.
Heian International, Union City, CA, 1990.

Lip, Evelyn. FENG SHUI: A LAYMAN'S GUIDE TO CHINESE GEOMANCY.
Heian International, Union City, CA, 1979.

O'Brien, Joanne with Kwok Man Ho. THE ELEMENTS OF FENG SHUI.
Element Books, Longmead, England, 1991.

Pennick, Nigel. THE ANCIENT SCIENCE OF GEOMANCY: LIVING IN HARMONY WITH THE EARTH.
CRCS Publications, Sebastopol, CA, 1979.

Rossbach, Sarah. FENG SHUI: THE ART OF CHINESE PLACEMENT.
E. P. Dutton, New York, NY, 1983.

Rossbach, Sarah. INTERIOR DESIGN WITH FENG SHUI.
E. P. Dutton, New York, NY, 1987.

Skinner, Stephen. THE LIVING EARTH MANUAL OF FENG-SHUI.
Routledge, Kegan Paul, London, England, 1982.

Walters, Derek. FENG SHUI: THE CHINESE ART OF DESIGNING A HARMONIOUS ENVIRONMENT.
Fireside Books, Simon and Schuster, New York, NY, 1988.

Walters, Derek. CHINESE GEOMANCY.
Element Books, Longmead, England, 1989.

Walters, Derek. THE FENG SHUI HANDBOOK.
Aquarian Press, London, England, 1991.

Works Relating to Chinese Philosophy

Blofeld, John (translation and commentary). **I CHING, THE BOOK OF CHANGE.**
E. P. Dutton, New York, NY, 1968.

Chan, Wing-Tsit (translation and compilation). **A SOURCE BOOK IN CHINESE PHILOSOPHY.**
Princeton University Press, Princeton, NJ, 1969.

Chang, Chung-yuan. TAO: A NEW WAY OF THINKING
(translation and commentary upon the *Tao Te Ching)*.
Perennial Library, Harper and Row, New York, NY, 1975.

Chia, Mantak and Maneewan Chia. FUSION OF THE FIVE ELEMENTS.
Healing Tao Books, Huntington, NY, 1989.

Dhiegh, Khigh Alex. THE ELEVENTH WING: AN EXPOSITION OF THE DYNAMICS OF THE I CHING FOR NOW.
Delta Books, Dell Publishing, New York, NY, 1973.

Fung, Yu-Lan (Derk Bodde, editor). A SHORT HISTORY OF CHINESE PHILOSOPHY.
Free Press Paperback, Macmillan Company, New York, NY, 1948.

Henricks, Robert G. (translation and commentary). **LAO TZU TE TAO CHING.**
Ballantine Books, New York, NY, 1989.

Legge, James (translation and commentary). **THE I CHING, THE BOOK OF CHANGES.**
Dover Publications, New York, NY, 1899, 1963.

Lin, Yutang (translation, editing, and commentary). **THE WISDOM OF LAOTSE.**
The Modern Library, Random House, New York, NY, 1948, 1976.

Wilhelm, Helmut. HEAVEN, EARTH AND MAN IN THE BOOK OF CHANGES.
University of Washington Press, Seattle, WA, 1977.

Wilhelm, Richard (translation: Chinese to German and commentary), **Carl F. Baynes** (translation: German to English). **THE I CHING OR BOOK OF CHANGES.**
Bolligen Series XIX, Princeton University Press, Princeton, NJ, 1950.

Works Relating to the Ways (*Tao* or *Do*)

Chang, Stephen. THE COMPLETE BOOK OF ACUPUNCTURE.
Celestial Arts, Milbrae, CA, 1976.

Cleary, Thomas (translation). THE ART OF WAR by SUN TZU.
Shambhala, Boston, MA, 1988.

Herrigel, Eugene. ZEN IN THE ART OF ARCHERY.
Vintage Books, Random House, New York, NY, 1953.

Kaptchuk, Ted. THE WEB THAT HAS NO WEAVER: UNDER-STANDING CHINESE MEDICINE.
Congdon and Weed, New York, NY, 1983.

Legett, Trevor. ZEN AND THE WAYS.
Shambhala, Boulder, CO, 1978.

Miyamoto, Mushashi (Victor Harris, translation). A BOOK OF FIVE RINGS.
The Overlook Press, Woodstock, NY, 1974.

O'Brien, John and Dan Bensky (translation). ACUPUNCTURE: A COMPREHENSIVE TEXT, SHANGHAI COLLEGE OF TRADITIONAL CHINESE MEDICINE.
Eastland Press, Seattle, WA, 1981.

Omori, Sogen and Terayama Katsujo (John Stevens, translation). ZEN AND THE ART OF CALLIGRAPHY: THE ESSENCE OF SHO.
Routledge, Kegan Paul, London, England, 1983.

Stryk, Lucien. ENCOUNTER WITH ZEN: WRITINGS ON POETRY AND ZEN. Swallow Press, Ohio University Press, Chicago, IL, 1981.

Suzuki, Daisetz. ZEN AND JAPANESE CULTURE.
Bolligen Series LXIV, Princeton University Press, Princeton, NJ, 1959, 1973.

Tohei, Koichi. BOOK OF KI: CO-ORDINATING MIND AND BODY IN DAILY LIFE.
Japan Publications, Inc., Tokyo, Japan, 1976.

Wright, Tom and Mizuno Katsuhiko. ZEN GARDENS: KYOTO'S NATURE ENCLOSED.
Suiko Books, Kyoto, Japan, 1990.

Yuan, Gao. LURE THE TIGER OUT OF THE MOUNTAINS: 36 STRATAGEMS OF ANCIENT CHINA.
Simon and Schuster, New York, NY, 1991.

Works Relating to Western and Chinese Astrological Systems

Chu, W. K. (translation), **W. A. Sherril** (editing and commentary). **THE ASTROLOGY OF THE I CHING (HO MAP LO MAP RATIONAL NUMBER MANUSCRIPT).**
Samuel Weiser, Inc., New York, NY, 1976.

Cozzi, Steve. PLANETS IN LOCALITY: EXPLORING LOCAL SPACE ASTROLOGY.
Llewellyn Publications, St. Paul, MN, 1988.

Gagne, Steve and John Mann. THE NINE KI HANDBOOK: AN UPDATED GUIDE TO NINE STAR KI ASTROLOGY.
Spiralbound Books, Rochester, NY, 1985.

Kriyananda, Goswami. THE WISDOM AND WAY OF ASTROLOGY.
Temple of Kriya Yoga, Chicago, IL, 1974, 1985.

Lau, Theodora. THE HANDBOOK OF CHINESE HOROSCOPES.
Colophon Books, Harper and Row, New York, NY, 1979.

Palmer, Martin, Kwok Man-Ho and Kerry Brown. THREE LIVES: A PRACTICAL CHINESE GUIDE TO REINCARNATION.
Century Paperbacks, London, England, 1987.

Walters, Derek. CHINESE ASTROLOGY.
The Aquarian Press, Thomas Publishing Group, Wellingborough, England, 1987.

Walters, Derek. MING SHU: THE ART AND PRACTICE OF CHINESE ASTROLOGY.
Fireside Books, Simon and Schuster, New York, NY, 1987.

Moon

Feng Shui Consultations

Harmony with Tao, the Great Way of the Universe, is the aim of the art of *feng shui,* known as the Way of Wind and Water. The focus of *feng shui* is re-creation of harmony in the space between heaven and earth, filled by the landscape and by the acts, dreams and buildings of man. How to recognize imbalance and restore natural and primordial harmony is the method of the art. How to create conscious, elevating change is its fruit. The aim, focus, method and fruit of the art are applied through a *feng shui* consultation.

Feng shui, as the art of living, means constant cultivation of self for both *feng shui* master and sponsor. The *feng shui* master is a facilitator, urging you to become the creator of your own life, not the inhabitant of a bundle of habitual routines, negative emotions and untested beliefs. The *I Ching* calls this self-transformation process "becoming a dragon." Applying the art of *feng shui* to your home or business with a *feng shui* master will reveal where you are in this process.

Diagnosis is the first step in a *feng shui* consultation. Diagnosis in the art of *feng shui* is the means of seeing the nature of the universe intimately, knowing yourself in the same way, and expressing both in your surroundings. Every wall, decoration, piece of furniture or art work where you live should radiate the vitality of this expression. If it doesn't, it means that to a large extent, you have become the prisoner of other peoples' values, sensibilities, or dreams of power. Through *feng shui* diagnosis, the master discovers the active limits to your freedom and the strength of the entrapping forces.

A *Feng Shui* Prescription

A *feng shui* consultation includes diagnosis, prescription of cures and re-creation. It includes clear seeing, a compassionate dialogue and a commitment to change. The prescription of *feng shui* cures is the means to re-create your home or business as you remodel, redo and rearrange your life pattern toward the attainment of your life goals. A *feng shui* prescription is really a plan by which you refocus your life objectively, subjectively and ritually, the result of a dialogue with a *feng shui* master.

Cures can include changes to your home or business, changes in your life patterns, or changes in your internal "architecture." Each *feng shui* cure is calculated to produce a positive and liberating counterforce to dissolve negative influences found in the diagnosis. Envisioning cures is the second part of any *feng shui* consultation.

Re-creation in *feng shui* means you must empower yourself creatively toward attaining your life goals. The third part of the consultation really is your work, although it contains some encouragement from the *feng shui* master. It happens as you visibly focus your life, in your home or office, enact the cures, and reaffirm them daily and consciously. To achieve your goals will require perseverance. You may have to recast everything in your home or office environment many times to achieve what you want in balance with the Tao.

There are tens of millions of ways to change your life. There are thousands of positive directions to take. But there are less than fifty conscious and harmonious ways to elevate yourself toward genuine contentment. *Feng shui* is one of these few ways, which is why a *feng shui* consultation is so valuable.

Time and space are the two greatest limitations of our human experience. *Feng shui* can turn these vast obstructions into great opportunities. *Feng shui* is the art of positioning in time and space, so it shows you how to flow in the time-and-space ocean that carries you adrift in its currents. A *feng shui* consultation shows you how your neighborhood, front gate or office desk places you in nuturing or destructive currents. It can show you how to make overlooked energies work for you rather than against you, which can make all the difference in your performance, result and reward.

Services Offered Through *Daikakuji*

Daikakuji means Great Enlightenment Temple. In the post-modern world, a Temple in the Zen Buddhist tradition is a skillful combination of ways to lead a person to enlightened mind. Specifically, *Daikakuji* publishes books and tapes about *feng shui, qi gong,* and Zen practice. Building and life change rituals also are provided through *Daikakuji* as a companion to some *feng shui* consultations. *Daikakuji* also sponsors a *feng shui deshi* training program. The *deshi* program is an intensive apprenticeship study combining tapes, practical projects, in-person seminars and individual guidance. As the *deshi*-teacher relation grows over the introductory nine month study period, some students will be invited to join more thorough *feng shui* studies leading to course completion in three years.

Daikakuji
Post Office Box 44035
Phoenix, AZ 85064-4035
Phone: (602) 788-3398

Govert Zengo Design Services

Feng shui consultations for home, business and corporate life are available through Govert Zengo Design by Johndennis Govert and his Associates. Consultations are more effectively done in person; however, consultations by phone are sometimes possible, especially in the follow-up planning and construction phases of building projects. If you are thinking of building anew or remodeling, the easier and more cost-effective time to consider a *feng shui* consultation is at the planning stage. An even better time is the moment before you select a building site.

The subtle arts of *feng shui* navigated through the limits and possibilities of the modern, Western building process is a service Govert Zengo Design uniquely offers. Remodeling and construction involve a complex set of interrelations among architects, contractors, interior designers, landscape designers, suppliers, City and County building and zoning regulators -- all of whom greatly impact how dream homes or successful business establishments can be built. Govert Zengo Design works very well with this process to facilitate creative *feng shui* solutions that coalesce your whole design team so that together we more effectively attune your place more closely to realize your life goals.

Please call 602-788-3398 for more information.

About the Author

Johndennis Govert holds an MBA in strategic planning and organizational change from Northwestern University. He has twenty-one years in this field, often advising clients of architectural as well as strategic business planning. He is the co-founder and first President of the Northwest Institute of Acupuncture and Oriental Medicine in Seattle. He is a *Soto* Zen priest, holder of the *Roshi*, or Master degree, and founder of *Daikakuji* — Great Enlightenment Temple. Govert-*Roshi* teaches classes and leads retreats in Zen meditation, *qi gong*, Western astrology, Oriental philosophy and *Feng Shui Tao*. Johndennis Govert is a warm, knowledgeable, humorous, and compassionate guide to the wisdom traditions of the East practically applied to home and business life in the West.

For more information, or to arrange a consultation or a class, please contact:

Johndennis Govert
Daikakuji
Post Office Box 44035
Phoenix, AZ 85064-4035
Phone: (602) 788-3398
Fax: (602) 788-8555

Glossary of *Feng Shui Tao* Terms

Terms defined in the glossary are for your convenience and come from various Asian languages. The language key is Chinese (CHN), Japanese (JPN), Sanskrit (SKT), and Tibetan (TBT). The abbreviations identify the language of origin.

Aikido: (JPN) A martial art founded by Morihei Ueshiba called "Way of Harmonious Energy." The cultivation and use of *ki* is central to this art.

Aum mani padme hung: (SKT/TBT) "Hail to the Jewel in the Lotus!" This is a *mantra* invoking *Avalokiteshvara*, *Boddhisattva* of Compassion and inner compassion.

Ba gua: (CHN) The eight signs or trigrams of the *I Ching* representing eight natural and primal forces shaping the world.

Boddhisattva: (SKT) An enlightened being who remains in the cycle of human existence to help humans evolve.

Buddhism: (SKT) A mystical practice concerned with cultivating Enlightenment. It began in India and was transmitted throughout Asia. It is one of the three great philosophical schools of China.

Bushido: (JPN) The Way of the Warrior. It encompasses all the martial arts of Japan.

Chado: (JPN) "The Way of Tea" begun by Zen Masters *Eisai* and later *Ikkyu*. It is also known as Tea Ceremony.

Ch'an: (CHN) The "Meditation School" of Buddhism in China. See *Zen*.

Daikakuji: (JPN) The Great Enlightenment Temple in Phoenix, founded by Govert *Roshi*.

Dharma: (SKT) "Universal law, duty, things." In both Vedic and Buddhist traditions, the teachings on the nature of universal law and the method of how to transform and transcend the small self.

Do: (JPN) The Way, a road. See *Tao*.

Enso: (JPN) A circle drawn in calligraphy to represent the oneness of all life and to express intimate and immediate connection with the origin.

Feng Shui Tao: (CHN) The Way of Wind and Water, an ancient geomantic art and a method for self-cultivation.

Genkan: (JPN) "Dark Hall." It is a foyer in traditional Japanese homes and buildings.

Gua (sometimes *kua*): (CHN) Refers to one of eight trigrams or one of the sixty-four hexagrams found in the I Ching.

Hiragana: (JPN) System of Japanese phonetic characters used for writing native Japanese words.

Huang Ti: (CHN) The Yellow Emperor. The legendary first Emperor of China from the start of whose reign the Chinese years are reckoned (Chinese year 4691 is 1993).

Iaido: (JPN) "The Way of the Sword." Training is only with a live *samurai* sword. Compare with *Kendo*.

I Ching: (CHN) THE BOOK OF CHANGE, the oldest writing in China on philosophy, divination, culture and self-development.

Ikebana: (JPN) "The Way of Flower Arranging." Many schools of this art flourish in Japan.

Jing-lo: (CHN) The system of meridians and energy flow of *qi* used in acupuncture and Chinese herbal medicine.

Kado: (JPN) "The Way of Poetry." Writing of *haiku* and *renga* poem styles to deepen awareness and appreciation of nature.

Kanji: (JPN) Chinese ideographic characters drawn with brush and ink.

Katakana: (JPN) System of Japanese phonetic characters used for writing foreign words from English, German, Dutch, etc.

Kendo: (JPN) "The Way of the Sword." Now practiced with bamboo swords. Compare with *Iaido.*

Ki: (JPN) Same as *Qi. Ki* is concentrated in the *hara,* the area below the navel.

Ki ga aru! (JPN) "Life energy exists!"

Kung Fu Tzu: (CHN) Master Kung Fu, also known as Confucius, founder of one of the three great philosophical schools of China.

Kyudo: (JPN) "The Way of Archery." The use of bow and arrow as a way to self-awareness and cultivation.

Laoshi: (CHN) "Old Teacher," a title of respect. See *Roshi.* Pronounced differently, it means honest or frank.

Lao Tzu: (CHN) "Old Master." It refers to the author of the *Tao Te Ching* and founder of Taoism, one of the three great philosophical schools of China.

Luo Pan: (CHN) A *feng shui* compass used by the cosmological school.

Lung: (TBT) See *qi.*

Mahayana: (SKT) "Great Vehicle." A branch of Buddhist practice that extols the attainment of enlightenment not only to relieve one's own suffering, but as a means to liberate and help others as well.

Mandala: (SKT) "Circle, orb." A symbolic seed representation in the center of a circular figure surrounded by concentric symbols showing how the universe is ordered. It is used in art or visualization meditation to enter into greater harmony or integration with the One.

Mantra: (SKT) Sound vibrations to invoke positive and transforming thought-forms, and to invoke internal and external states.

Mantrayana: (SKT) "Mantra Vehicle." Any Mystic school relying mainly on mantra practice, or recitation of a verbal sound formula. Also refers to Tibetan Tantric Buddhism.

Ming Shu: (CHN) System of Chinese astrology connected to *feng shui* in the *luo pan.*

Mu: (JPN) See *wu.*

Norin: (JPN) An artful doorway drape much used as decoration in Japan.

Origami: (JPN) The art of folding paper into animate, inanimate and man-made forms. This is also a Chinese art form.

Pinyin: (CHN) A modern system for writing Chinese words in Roman letters.

Prana: (SKT) See *qi.*

Qi: (CHN) Sometimes written *ch'i.* Basic life energy that flows through the body and the whole universe and mediates change between physical matter and emotional and mental realms. Also referred to as *ki, lung* and *prana.*

Qi gong: (CHN) (Also *Ch'i Gung* or *Ch'i Kung*) Practice of internal exercises that promote accumulation and circulation of *qi* in the physical, astral and causal bodies. An indispensable practice in order to master any of the Ways.

River Lo Map: (CHN) Also known as the River Lo Writing, it is an ancient written text used in the *yin-yang* school of Chinese philosophy.

Romaji: (JPN) "Roman letters." Refers to Japanese words written with English letters.

Roshi: (JPN) "Old Teacher." It is the same *kanji* as the Chinese *laoshi,* but in the Zen Buddhist school, the title takes on the connotation of "Zen Master."

Samadhi: (SKT) "Complete, eternal, absorption." Balanced self-conscious awareness, the state of enlightenment.

Satori: (JPN) Deep and sudden realization of the true nature of things.

Sensei: (JPN) "Previous Birth." In Japan, it is a respectful title that simply means teacher whether of kindergarten, *ikebana, aikido* or Zen. Compare with *xiansheng.*

Sha qi: (CHN) Energies directed at a site or running through a site that injure or overwhelm those who live or work there.

Shodo: (JPN) "The Way of Calligraphy." Refers to the art of brush and ink writing of *kanji,* Chinese characters.

Soto: (JPN) "Mount *Ts'ao* and Mount *Tung.*" Two Zen masters and their monasteries in *Tang* China (900 A.D.), where one of the five schools of Zen originated. The five sects are *Soto (Ts'ao Tung); Rinzai (Lin Chi); Hogen (Fa Yen); Ummon (Yun Men);* and *Ikyo (Wei Yang). Soto* Zen emphasizes silent illumination meditation.

Sume-i: (JPN) A type of brush and ink (black and gray) painting of natural subjects.

Sun Tzu: (CHN) "Master Sun." Military strategist and author of THE ART OF WAR, the most influential writing on the strategy of war in China.

Tai Ji Tu: (CHN) "The Supreme Ultimate." The symbol of *yin* and *yang* joined in dynamic union within the One. Represents before and after first Creation.

Tan Tien (CHN) or *Tanden* (JPN): "Heavenly Field." Refers to psychic and energy centers of the body. The three principal *tan tien* are the navel, heart and between the eyes, but can refer to others, including the acupuncture points.

Tao: (CHN) "The Way." The mysterious and subtle origin, the pre-Creation reality and self-cultivation following the Great Way of the universe. May also refer to an individual Way such as poetry, tea or *feng shui.*

Tao Te Ching: (CHN) "THE CLASSIC OF THE WAY AND ITS POWER," a work attributed to *Lao Tzu;* the first written work in the Chinese Taoist school.

Taoism: (CHN) One of China's three great philosophical schools. Taoism has philosophical, mystical practice and religious sub-schools, based on *Lao Tzu's* teachings in the poems of the *Tao Te Ching.*

Tokunoma: (JPN) An alcove near the entry of Japanese buildings and in important rooms in which calligraphy or painted scrolls, *ikebana* arrangements or art works are displayed prominently.

Vajrayana: (SKT) "Diamond Vehicle." A branch of Buddhist practice to transform and cut through human delusion to reveal enlightened mind. This Buddhism includes Chinese "Secret Sect," most of the Tibetan Buddhist sects and Japanese *Shingon.*

Wade-Giles: (CHN) An older, alternate system for writing Chinese word sounds with English letters. See *Pinyin.*

Wu: (CHN) "Emptiness." Refers to the fundamental character of life that is so deep as to be fathomless, but which can be applied to connect humankind harmoniously with all creation. See *kanji* on last page.

Wu Xing: (CHN) "The Five Agents." Refers to the five basic processes at work making the world including wood, fire, earth, metal and water.

Xiansheng: (CHN) "Previous Birth," or "Previous Being." Title meaning Master of a particular Way, art or trade. It is reserved for great accomplishment. Although it is the same *kanji* as the Japanese *"Sensei,"* the connotations are quite different.

Yang: (CHN) "Banners waving in the sun." One of two penultimate powers emanating from the One (see *Tai Ji Tu*) Also means "district of light." Always paired with *yin.*

Yin: (CHN) "Cloudy, obscure." One of the two penultimate powers emanating from the One *(Tai Ji Tu).* Also means "district of darkness." Always paired with *yang.*

Zazen: (JPN) "Sitting meditation." Refers to a method of meditation practiced by the *Zen* Buddhist school of Japan. Also known as *shikantaza* — only sitting, and *mokushozen* — meditation of silent illumination.

Zen: (JPN) *Mahayana* "Meditation" school of Buddhism transmitted from India to China, then to Japan in the 13th Century A.D. in the *Rinzai, Soto* and *Obaku* sects.

Zendo: (JPN) "The Way of Zen." Refers to the practice of meditation in the Zen tradition. Sometimes may refer to the hall in which Zen meditation is practiced.

Wu